Murder in Lancashire

A New Look at Notorious Cases

ALAN SEWART

ROBERT HALE · LONDON

© *Alan Sewart 1988*
First published in Great Britain 1988

Robert Hale Limited
Clerkenwell House
Clerkenwell Green
London EC1R 0HT

British Library Cataloguing in Publication Data

Sewart, Alan
    Murder in Lancashire : a new look at
    notorious cases.
    1. Lancashire. Murder, 1820–1988
    I. Title
    364.1'523'094276

    ISBN 0-7090-3561-6

Photoset in North Wales by
Derek Doyle & Associates, Mold, Clwyd.
Printed in Great Britain by
St Edmundsbury Press Ltd, Bury St Edmunds, Suffolk.
Bound by Woolnough Bookbinding Ltd.

Contents

For my wife – who reads
everything I write.

Acknowledgements

The Chief Constable of Lancashire, Brian Johnson QPM, gave me his blessing and the key to his archives. His officers at all levels showed me how – and where – to look, and brought cases to my notice that I might otherwise have missed.

The Clerk of the Peace for the county steered me towards the Lancashire Record Office, where an obliging staff fed me with the most crucial historical information.

Officials at Blackburn Reference Library advised and helped me.

The Bury Times, Bolton Evening News and *Blackburn Telegraph* allowed me access to ancient, crumbling, yellowed pages from the past. Other newspapers – *The Times, The Guardian, The Daily Mail, The Preston Chronicle and Lancashire Advertiser, The Wigan Observer, The Lancashire Daily Post, The Nelson Gazette, The West Lancashire Evening Gazette, The Barking and Dagenham Independent* and others not identifiable – supplied unwitting help in the form of cuttings attached to various files.

My grateful thanks go to all these benefactors, known and unknown.

MURDER IN LANCASHIRE

0   5   10 miles

0   5   10   15 km

Settle

Morecambe
Lancaster

LANCASHIRE

Slaidburn

Ribchester
Ann Walne

Nelson
Ruth Clarkson

Colne

Fleetwood

Garstang

Broughton
William Openshaw

Longridge

Blackburn
Emily Holland

Burnley

Blackpool

M55

Preston

Accrington
Sarah Coates

St Annes-on-sea
*Kathleen H.E.
Breaks*

Charnock Richard
Eric L.W. Renton

M6

Darwen
Naomi Annie Farnworth

Rochdale

Southport

Knowsley
*Douglas Stuart
Walter Stallard*

Ormskirk

Tottington
Samuel Hutton

Bury   M62

M61   Bolton

Oldham

Huyton
*Paula Louisa
Atkinson*

M58

Wigan
Robert Kidd

Manchester

Hollinwood
Sarah McCrinn

M57

St Helens

Liverpool   M62

Old Trafford
Nicholas Cock

M6

THE NAMES OF THE VICTIMS ARE SHOWN IN ITALIC BELOW THE PLACE NAMES

Introduction

'When Mr Gillette invented the safety razor in 1895, he changed the pattern of murder.'

Not my words, but those of Joe Mounsey, Assistant Chief Constable of Lancashire, who knows more than most about murder. And how apt they proved when I began to delve into the bloody history of this, the most serious and the most fascinating of crimes, committed in the Red Rose County over the past 160 years. Pre-1900, the open razor was a very popular murder weapon. After that time, much less so.

But throat-slitting and mystery seldom went hand in hand. In dozens and dozens of cases the killers were found beside the bodies of their victims, still clutching the razor, often dead or dying from having turned the same weapon on themselves.

Tragic events, but ordinary. For that reason the open razor figures only once in this anthology. It was used at Blackburn in 1876 (Chapter 11). And that crime was greater than mere throat-slitting. In the only parallel, at Huyton in 1963 (Chapter 10), a safety-razor blade was used.

Although women commit murder almost as frequently as men, generally speaking they are less disposed to guile, and with a few exceptions their victims are close relatives or associates – the commonly termed 'domestic' murders.

That is why almost all my murderers are men. The single exception is found in Chapter 14 – and whether or not Elizabeth Hutton poisoned her son is the mystery in that instance.

I could have chosen more notorious crimes: Doctor Buck Ruxton, Brady and Hindley, the 'handless corpse' case and Donald Neilson, fancifully dubbed 'The Black Panther', who killed at least once in Lancashire. I opted for cases less well known but not – I believe – less interesting.

A.S.

1 The Darwen Child Murder, Darwen 1932

> Between the hills so bleak and barren,
> Lies the town of dirty Darren.

There is a road, the A666, which runs from the cotton capital of Manchester, scene of the famous Peterloo Massacre, to the wild district around Pendle Hill, historic home of the Lancashire Witches, as chronicled by Harrison Ainsworth.

Along this road tramcars clanked, rattled and flashed until after the Second World War, when the spread of the motor bus brought the tramcar era virtually to an end. Today the A666 remains a trunk road, even busier than before, curling like a warped spear aimed from the heart of Lancashire at the heart of Yorkshire. If one follows it from Bolton to Blackburn, one is bound to pass through the smaller town of Darwen, in origin principally a cotton town but home also of paper-making, coal-mining and stone-quarrying.

It is difficult to conceive of a more terse yet complete description of Darwen than that contained in the above couplet by an unknown wag who was also a poet. He cannot, by the way, be faulted for his spelling. In proper usage the 'w' in Darwen is not silent, but in the vernacular – now, as then – the town's name rhymes perfectly with 'barren', and most of its inhabitants still call themselves 'Darreners'.

Darwen is long and narrow, a classic example of ribbon development. It lies in a deep cleft of the Pennine foothills and seems hemmed in by bleak and barren slopes. On certain side streets built at right angles to the road there are terraces of houses whose roofs rise in series, one above the other like flights of giant stairs, and to climb to the tops of these streets, carrying shopping bags or wheeling perambulators, must have been a daunting chore for many brave hearts until the motor car took the sting away.

In describing Darwen as 'dirty', the couplet is not so much inaccurate as out of date. There was a time, and not so long ago, when it would not have been defamatory to describe the whole of industrial Lancashire in those terms, when King Cotton ruled everywhere and the massive mill chimneys poured their clouds of filth into the atmosphere. Today most of those chimneys have been demolished, and the combined effects of the Clean Air Acts and modern light industry have made the town a cleaner, brighter place. And Darwen can even claim to be a forerunner in the progress race. As early as 1930, this town of some 36,000 souls could boast one of the finest Olympic-sized public swimming-baths in the area. It was erected in memory of the great Lancastrian Sir Robert Peel, thrice Prime Minister and founder of the 'New' (Metropolitan) Police, in 1829.

In 1918, when Mr and Mrs Cowle came to live there with their two small sons, Darwen must have offered a grimy, gloomy contrast with their previous home in Douglas, Isle of Man. But the family stayed, settling at 82 Kay Street. Charles James Cowle, their elder son, was five years old at the time, having been born in Douglas on 29 April 1913. He was still little more than a child (just nineteen, in fact) when, on Wednesday 18 May 1932, he was hanged at Strangeways Prison, Manchester, for the murder of Naomi Annie Farnworth, aged six. Annie Farnworth had lived next door but one, at 86 Kay Street.

But the short history of the crimes of Charles James Cowle begins earlier, in 1922. His first victim was Thomas Smith, then aged two years and two months, of 20 Garnett Street, Darwen.

About 4.30 p.m. on Monday 4 September 1922 the little boy was found sitting up to his waist in the waters of a brook at Ellison Fold, Darwen. He was seriously injured about the head, and it seems likely the child would have died if not found quickly. By lucky chance he was found in time.

Thomas Smith's grandmother, Mary Jane Clayton, of 25 Elswick Street, which is not far from Ellison Fold, had seen her grandson toddling in the direction of the stream accompanied by Cowle. Shortly afterwards she went to look for the child and came face to face with Cowle, who was leaving the place. She asked Cowle, 'Where's the little lad with the green frock?' and Cowle told her, 'He has fallen into some water down there and is bleeding.' Hurrying to the stream, she found Thomas, who could only say to her, 'Grandma. Lad.'

Prompt action by Mrs Clayton saved the child, and though he was very ill when he was seen by Acting Police Inspector Shimmin at Blackburn Infirmary, there was, in the words of house surgeon Dr Daniel Ivan Greasey, 'A chance of recovery if complications do not set in'.

Meantime, in actions which were to prove a close pattern with later events, Cowle was airing his knowledge of the matter with some pride. To Edith Wilson, a dressmaker, of Ellison Fold, he said, 'A big lad has pushed him in and hit him with a stone.' And to Bertha Pilkington, of 61 Kay Street, where he went for meals whilst his parents were at work, he said in more detail, 'A little lad has been thrown into some water by a man and the man threw a brick at him and cut his nose and a lady took the boy into their house and they have taken him to the hospital in a cab.'

By the time he was arrested by Inspector Shimmin, Cowle had changed his story a little. 'The lad fell in the brook,' he said. 'I had the brick in my hand and the brick slipped out of my hand and cut his face.'

Cowle was then just nine years old. In modern times, in view of his tender years, he could not have been held responsible for this attack, but in 1922 the case was different. He was charged with aggravated assault and on the 3 October 1922, at Darwen Police Court, he was found guilty and committed to an Industrial School for five years.

Lostock Industrial School, to which he was first committed, closed its doors in June 1924, and Cowle was transferred to the Boys' School at Offerton, Stockport. In view of what was to happen later, it is interesting to note certain written comments made by Arthur Binks, headmaster of Offerton School.

'Cowle,' Binks recorded, 'was mainly quiet. No serious illness. A loner, preferring to read rather than join in games. Tidy. Scrupulously clean. Considerably better behaved than most boys there. No abnormality.' Binks also commented that Cowle was 'very short' – he was four feet 5½ inches at the age of fourteen. He was, however, inclined to be stout.

There was no remission, it seems. Cowle completed his five years and was almost fifteen years old when he returned to live with his parents at 82 Kay Street, Darwen.

During his absence a happy event had occurred at the home of his near neighbours Albert and Henrietta Farnworth, and their daughter, Naomi Annie Farnworth, had reached the age of three. Cowle must have met the little girl shortly after his discharge from Offerton, and in the remaining three years of her life he came to know her well.

There was no question of Cowle's returning to an ordinary school. At almost fifteen and with no special abilities, he was too old for that. His working life was patchy and short, whether due to the serious economic depression of the time or to his own lack of industry cannot be said with certainty. He obtained a job as a labourer but left after four months, giving as his reason that he was flat-footed and, 'The work did not suit his feet.' Later he worked for three weeks as a cotton-piecer at New Mill, Union Street, Darwen, and latterly, for a few more weeks, again as a cotton-piecer, at Barlow & Jones' Mill, Edgworth, Bolton. He was discharged from there 'owing to bad trade' (nowadays it would be termed redundancy), and thereafter he was unemployed. He seems to have spent most of his later years hanging about in the vicinity of his home. However, he fared well enough, for both his parents were in work, and on the strength of their earnings he was allowed credit at the local fish and chip shop, run by Mrs Brunfitt. From her he regularly obtained tripe and chips or 'threepenny mixes' of chips and peas. Often he would induce local children to fetch his food for him, a fact which was to figure prominently in the investigation into the death of Annie Farnworth.

That first came to notice, as such incidents often do, when Annie Farnworth was reported missing from home. The girl was a pupil at Highfield Infant School in the town. Normally she attended there from 9 a.m. until 12 noon, when she would make her way to the nearby Vernon Street School for a meal provided free by the Darwen Education Authority for 'the children of unemployed and poor parents'. After the meal she usually, though not always, called briefly at her home before returning to Highfield School for the afternoon session, and then, when classes were over for the day she would go home fairly promptly.

On Tuesday 22 March 1932 Annie Farnworth was not seen at her home after the midday meal. As was later learned, however, she did go to Kay Street, where Cowle spoke to her and sent her to Brunfitts' chip shop to bring him his meal. She was seen at the shop by the proprietor and also by an older girl, Doris Sharples, aged thirteen. Annie was carrying a white jug known to be Cowle's, and she asked for 'A threepenny mix for Charlie Cowle.' She was told there were no peas left and was supplied with chips only, though at a later time Cowle was to say he had sent her for tripe.

There is little doubt that Mrs Brunfitt and Doris Sharples were the last persons apart from Cowle himself to see Annie Farnworth alive. When she carried the jug back to 82 Kay Street, Cowle enticed her into the house, ravished her, strangled her with a cord and thus, in the quaint wording of the subsequent charge, 'Wilfully and of his malice aforethought did kill and murder one Naomi Annie Farnworth, against the Peace of our Sovereign Lord The King, his Crown and Dignity'.

That he had done so was, of course, not known until later. And his own knowledge of the act seems not to have upset him. At 6 p.m. on the day of the crime, with the body of his victim hidden in the bedroom he shared with his parents, Cowle went next door to a house that abutted his own but which was actually in Elizabeth Street and there played dominoes with his friend, nineteen-year-old James Edward Foster.

The girl had been missed by then, but no serious alarm bells were ringing. Her father had begun to feel uneasy at her lateness and after walking the streets between home and school he began to call on relatives to ask after her. His enquiries were not blessed, so later in the evening he went to the local police station to report his daughter missing.

Hopes were high at that stage, since children are apt to stray and are often found safe and well after a time, but as the night lengthened and Annie had not been traced, the details were passed to adjoining police areas and the search was intensified. Annie was described as of fair complexion, with very fair hair and uneven teeth, wearing steel-rimmed spectacles, dressed in a brown coat with two brass buttons on the front, a blue frock, blue hat, fawn stockings and clogs – which were common footwear for children in those days. In the first circulation she was said to have been missing since 6 p.m. on 22 March, but in a later message the time was amended to 1.15 p.m. This new information followed an interview in the small hours of the following morning with the headmistress of Highfield School, who was able to say that Annie had not returned for the afternoon session.

Later that day the girl's description was broadcast on radio from the Manchester station of the BBC. This was not done as a routine matter but was agreed to as the result of a direct request from Annie's parents.

About 5 p.m. on 23 March, in a show of bravado reminiscent of his actions after the earlier case, Cowle spoke to the girl Doris Sharples on the corner of Kay Street and Elizabeth Street (directly outside his home, in fact), saying: 'Have you heard about that little girl being lost?' Doris Sharples agreed that she had, whereupon Cowle said to her: 'You will be the next.'

Shortly after that he went into the home of his friend James Edward Foster, announced his intention of helping in the search for the missing girl and invited Foster to go with him. They joined other volunteers and searched round the St Johns district of Darwen and also through Sunnyhurst Wood, a not quite so bleak and barren section of those enclosing hills.

Gradually, as they went about their work, the police were piecing together a clearer picture of the missing girl's last known movements. At 9.45 a.m. on Thursday 24 March, ostensibly as part of routine house-to-house enquiries, two police constables interviewed Cowle at his home. He was quite ready to admit that on the day of her disappearance he had asked Annie Farnworth to fetch him some tripe and chips from Brunfitts' chip shop. After bringing them she had stayed in the house 'only a few minutes' and, according to Cowle, had then 'gone away'.

The constables recorded a short statement which Cowle signed, and then, as though satisfied, they left.

The reasons for what happened next have to be a matter for conjecture, but it can be imagined that the police had by this time formed their own opinions about Cowle. It would not have escaped their notice that he was on record as a violent person, and that fact, combined with his admission of having been with Annie around the material time, must have removed most of their remaining doubts. Within the hour there was a second visit to 82 Kay Street, this time by Inspector Kay and Detective Sergeant Kenyon. The story Cowle told them was substantially the same as before, except in relation to the period Annie had spent in the house. This time, Cowle said she had been there 'about twenty minutes', which would certainly have meant that she would be late for school.

'We don't believe you,' Inspector Kay said, 'and we're going to search this house.'

The announcement must have caused Cowle considerable alarm at a time when he was running out of bluff. As the two officers separated to begin searching the downstairs rooms, he followed Inspector Kay into the kitchen and there said, 'She's upstairs.' He led the officers up to the shared bedroom where he pointed to a metal trunk and said, 'She's in there. I strangled her.'

What the officers saw on lifting the lid of the trunk is perhaps best described in the words of the police surgeon, Dr W.E. Cooke, of Wigan, who examined the body, took possession of clothing from both victim and accused for microscopic examination and also conducted the subsequent post-mortem examination.

The body, Dr Cooke reported, had been placed in a tin trunk with the face uppermost. The thighs were flexed on the abdomen and the legs flexed on the thighs. The thighs were abducted (held apart). The elbows were semi-flexed with hands clenched. The lower abdomen and thighs were naked. Clothing on the body consisted of frock, petticoat, woollen vest, stockings and clogs. There was a cord around the neck: five coils, of which four were drawn tight, the fifth slacker. The cord, when later removed, measured six feet six inches.

Rigor mortis was present in thighs and legs but had almost passed off from arms and hands and was absent in the neck. There was some bruising on the arms, and blood/mucous in the mouth, also slight abrasions on the lips and a bruise the size of a threepenny piece (a new halfpenny, say) on the tongue.

The condition of the girl's genitals was ample evidence that intercourse had taken place – and by force. The presence of blood and spermatozoa confirmed that point, and staining of a like kind on the clothing of the accused man provided a useful link. In his final report, Dr Cooke expressed the firm opinion that death had been caused by strangulation, following rape.

Cowle himself consented to medical examination by his own doctor. The result was not particularly significant, but one remark by Dr John Willet provides an interesting comparison with earlier findings: 'Cowle's body was generally dirty,' the doctor reported. It will be recalled that Arthur Binks, headmaster of the Boys' School, Offerton, had once said of Cowle, 'He was scrupulously clean.'

A more detailed search of Cowle's bedroom revealed the dead girl's knickers, coat and hat in a small suitcase, and a bloodstained blanket on his bed. These things, taken with the presence of the body in the trunk for almost two days, give rise to speculation about an incidental but remarkable feature of the case. As pointed out earlier, Cowle shared a bedroom with his parents, and they might easily have come upon the body or clothing. His mother used the trunk for storing personal items and might have decided to open it at any time. Though it is clear she did not do so during those two days, one is left wondering what might have been the outcome if she had.

What had begun as a 'missing from home' was now known to be murder, and as a matter of routine the Divisional Commander, Superintendent Straits, informed the Lancashire Police Detective Department at Preston. Detective Chief Superintendent Gregson came to Darwen, but since Cowle was already in custody the chief superintendent's role was merely supervisory. It was Detective Sergeant Kenyon who charged Cowle with murder. Cowle's reply – no doubt inspired by the customary warning, 'Do you wish to say anything ...' given at time of charging – must have seemed a cliché even in those days and has certainly been used many times since.

'I have nothing to say,' he said.

The police surgeon did have something to say, even before the trial and its outcome. A handwritten letter from Dr Cooke to the chief constable, dated 6 April 1932, provides an interesting reminder of the vast effort which goes into any investigation of this kind and which inevitably is unrecorded and therefore unsung.

'My dear Chief Constable,' he writes. 'The police (lower) court proceedings in the Darwen murder case were completed today and I feel that I must say a word in appreciation of the efficiency with which the case was handled from Superintendent Straits down to the shorthand typists. Masterly is the only word that occurs to me to describe the superintendent's conduct of the case. To Inspector Kay and Detective Sergeant Kenyon I offer my congratulations on the brilliant piece of work which led to the arrest ...'

The trial itself was almost a formality. Long before it took place, the tactics of the defence, if not officially known, were at least anticipated. The facts would not be disputed, but the mental condition of Cowle would be put at issue in an effort to negative criminal responsibility.

'I have instructed Mr Roebuck to take charge of the case on my behalf,' wrote the Director of Public Prosecutions in a preliminary letter; he added, almost as an afterthought, 'I assume the usual enquiries are in hand to ascertain if there is any insanity in the history of the youth or his blood relations.'

Such enquiries *were* in hand.

There was no evidence of insanity in Cowle himself, but his paternal grandfather had been a voluntary patient for some months in Kirk Bradden Asylum, Isle of Man, and his maternal grandmother 'went funny' just before she died at the age of fifty-two. Also the paternal grandfather's half-sister and half-brother had been admitted to the Kirk Bradden Asylum and died there. The only other family skeleton at the time of the case was Cowle's younger brother, John James, who was an inmate of the Fylde Farm Approved School, committed there for dishonesty.

The mental specialist called to give evidence in Cowle's defence at the trial stated that Cowle was a high-grade mental defective who at the time of the offence was in a frenzy of sadistic lust.

This evidence seems to have cut no ice with the court, although the judge, Mr Justice Humphreys, did give assurance that any question of Cowle's age and mental condition would be considered by the proper authorities.

So, at Manchester Assizes on 26 April 1932, Cowle was found guilty and sentenced to death. The sight of the judge's black cap and his pronouncement that Cowle had been guilty of 'a terribly sadistic murder' seems to have caused him little unease.

According to a report in the *Lancashire Daily Post* of Wednesday 18 May, 'Unmoved when sentence of death was passed, he is said to have remarked to his father in an interview immediately afterwards, "What are you bothering about, Dad? I'm all right." '

Cowle, it was reported, had actually put on weight while living in the condemned cell.

The same report carried the news of his execution at Strangeways Gaol, Manchester, on 18 May (by the renowned executioner Albert Pierpoint), and of the formalities which always had to follow such a death: the certification and the posting of notices. 'Little public interest was shown,' the newspaper noted, 'and at the moment when Cowle went to the scaffold there were not more than 80 people waiting outside the main entrance to the prison. They mainly comprised unemployed men, but there were also a few women in shawls, some with children in arms or in perambulators.'

Nor, it seemed, was there much interest shown in Kay Street, Darwen, the scene of the murder, though it was noticed that the blinds were drawn at Cowle's home.

Three days later the Home Office issued a statement: 'In view of certain statements which have appeared in the press regarding the recent case of Charles James Cowle, who was convicted at the Lancashire Assizes of the murder of a girl of six years of age and who was executed on the 18th instant ...'. There followed a somewhat long-winded assurance that the Home Secretary had caused the necessary enquiries to be made under Section 2 (4) of the Criminal Lunatics Act, 1884, that the appointed medical practitioners did not consider Cowle to be insane or suffering from any other relevant mental abnormality and that as a result no grounds had arisen which would justify interference with the sentence.

Among the 'certain statements in the press' referred to by the Home Office was one attributed to a Mr Roy Calvert. It is perhaps the only one – I can find no other, and in view of its relevance to modern thinking it is worth quoting. Calvert's statement appeared in the *Lancashire Daily Post* of Wednesday 18 May immediately after the execution.

EXECUTION PROTEST
DECLARED TO BE 'AN OUTRAGE AGAINST
HUMANITY.'

This execution is an outrage against humanity. The Home Office has recently defended hanging for boys of 18 on the ground that motor bandits in their teens can be as wicked as those who are older. But Cowle was no motor bandit. He was a mental defective with the mental age of a child, and highly qualified medical evidence has been given that he was possessed of uncontrollable impulses. His was a horrible but meaningless crime. He was executed because our Courts still judge insanity by an 1843 definition, because few prison doctors are trained in mental diseases and because the Home Secretary inexplicably neglected to refer the case to a board of medical referees.

No doubt Calvert was a disappointed man who regarded Cowle's execution as yet another failure. In fact, as time would prove, it was another milestone on the path towards the reform he sought.

Roy Calvert was secretary of The National Council for the Abolition of the Death Penalty.

2 The Lamp of Enlightenment, Charnock Richard 1984

Among the exhibits in a small museum at the Lancashire Constabulary Training School is a brass lamp some nine inches high – a replica miners' safety lamp. A framed photograph of the same lamp hangs on the office wall of Detective Chief Superintendent Norman Finnerty, present head of CID.

This innocuous-looking object was not a murder weapon but the direct means of bringing a killer to book. The intriguing case in which it figured so prominently was an unusually fine illustration of the high standard of co-operation which exists between police forces as far apart as London and Edinburgh. In the course of the investigation, fingerprint evidence proved to be as useful as it has ever been in the detection of crime, the value of media publicity was highlighted, and a new Major Incident Room standardized administrative procedure was used effectively for the first time.

The murdered man, Eric Leslie Wandless Renton, lived alone in a bungalow at Charnock Richard near Chorley. The man who brutally killed him was a Yorkshireman, married in Scotland and living precariously in London. After committing the crime, this man stole property from the bungalow, piled it into the victim's car and drove to the London area, where he sold some of the property and abandoned the car. Later he disposed of the rest of the property to contacts in Scotland. He was well away from the scene before the murder was discovered, and before the police were anywhere near tracing him the stolen items were scattered far and wide.

The police net would have to spread just as widely.

But first a little more about the crime.

Eric Leslie Wandless was born at Bootle, Merseyside, on 3 December 1937. Nothing is known of his father. His mother died when he was only eight days old, and from that time he became an inmate of a National Children's Home at Frodsham, in Cheshire. At the age of fifteen he was adopted by Mrs Hilda Renton and assumed the surname by which he was later known. In 1979 Mrs Renton died, leaving him the bungalow at Charnock Richard and 'a considerable sum' of money. He used that money to purchase a small supermarket at 47 Windsor Road, Golborne, some eighteen miles from his home.

In some respects it could be said that Eric Renton fell foul of his own peculiar lifestyle. A bachelor, living alone, he was a self-confessed homosexual. He was in the habit of picking up male hitch-hikers and propositioning them for homosexual purposes. He had convictions for gross indecency. Since he was also a chess enthusiast, regularly attending tournaments as spectator or participant, much of his time away from business he spent travelling the main roads of the country in his car.

On Wednesday 11 January 1984 Renton's supermarket opened as usual but he did not go there. Used to his absences, his staff were not unduly concerned, but they did expect him to telephone, and when evening came and he had not done so, they began to be faintly worried. After the shop was closed for the day, Damion Bishop, aged eighteen, of Dursley, Gloucestershire, who was an employee and a friend, went to Renton's bungalow, 26 Neargates, Charnock Richard. Finding the house locked and in darkness he went to 14 Cunliffe Street, Chorley, the home of Frank Hughes, whom he knew as Renton's brother-in-law. Hughes had a key for the bungalow, and he and Bishop returned there, arriving at about 10.45 p.m. They unlocked the door, entered and went to the main bedroom. Renton's body was lying across the bed, naked apart from a bloodstained quilt over his legs. There were stab wounds in his chest and throat and a further serious wound to the head of the type usually attributed to a 'blunt instrument'.

Eric Renton was obviously dead. Hughes and Bishop withdrew in shock and sent for the police.

Detective Chief Inspector McClure and Detective Inspector Donald Biscomb went to the scene with other officers. The bedroom was generally untidy and the telephone wires had been broken at the socket. There was no obvious murder weapon, though there were knives in the house of various kinds. It is a reflection of the importance given to identifying a murder weapon that no fewer than fifty-three assorted knives and scissors were subsequently taken from the house for scientific examination. The body was examined *in situ* by the police surgeon Dr Martin Joseph Roche Ryan and forensic scientist Dr Frank Gore. In due course, when the scene had been thoroughly examined, sketched and photographed, the body was taken to the mortuary at the Royal Preston Hospital, where a post-mortem was later performed by Home Office pathologist Dr John Benstead.

Meanwhile a murder-incident room was quickly set up at Chorley police station, and Norman Finnerty, then a detective superintendent, was sent from headquarters to lead the investigation.

Enquiries soon revealed that Renton's car, a Ford Sierra, registered number A 201 HCK, was missing from the garage, and other property had been taken from the house. This included a television set, a video-recorder, a microwave oven, an alarm clock, a glass ash-tray and the replica miners' lamp. A description of all the missing property was circulated but in the initial stages priority was given to tracing the car.

On the afternoon of Thursday 12 January Terrence Anthony Lovekin of Dagenham, Essex, telephoned the police to complain that a strange car had been illegally parked in a 'residents only' area on the top floor of a multi-storey car-park near to his home. The car had first been seen earlier in the day by Lovekin's nine-year-old son, and Lovekin had waited for some time before calling the police.

The registered number was recognized at once, and the police at Dagenham knew they were dealing with something more serious than a mere parking problem. The car was examined by experts, and certain fingerprints were found. These proved to match other marks which by now had been found at the bungalow. Information was relayed to Lancashire. Detective Superintendent Finnerty, with thirty Lancashire officers, went at once to Dagenham and, with the full co-operation of the Metropolitan Police, set up a satellite incident room on the top floor of Barking police station.

The idea of running two incident rooms in tandem had not been tried before, and there were teething troubles. In the early stages there were no linked computer facilities, and vital information had to be passed between Dagenham and Chorley by land line, by road and even by post. But the satellite station functioned remarkably well and provided a model for later countrywide investigations.

With a great deal of help from Metropolitan officers, the men from Lancashire carried out high-density house-to-house enquiries, working in very harsh winter conditions, in their attempts to trace the person who had abandoned the Ford Sierra. More than 3,000 people were interviewed and their statements recorded – but all the effort seemed to be in vain.

Activity on this scale was unprecedented, and an item in *The Barking and Dagenham Independent* newspaper of the time drew attention to complaints about the excessive use in the district of officers from outside the area. In tone, the item was defensive of the police, but at one stage the reporter asked Norman Finnerty why it was necessary to have thirty of his men so engaged, not to mention the many others who must be working in the north. His reply must have surprised them. 'In Lancashire,' he said, 'we take murder very seriously.'

Perhaps they did but, as days passed, the break the officers were seeking did not materialize.

It was the Public Information Department at New Scotland Yard who made the suggestion that was to bring matters to a head. The list of stolen property, together with photographs of similar items, had been widely circulated already, but none of the items had turned up.

'Why not approach Shaw Taylor?' someone said.

And so they did. The well-known programme *Police Five* which was broadcast on ITV on Sunday 22 January 1984, carried an item dealing with the property missing in the Renton murder. Within minutes the police had their first real lead.

At 110 Salmon Lane, London, is a second-hand shop called 'San Fairy Anne'; proprietor, Elaine McDermott. Mrs McDermott watched the *Police Five* programme – and she remembered. Not so much about the man, perhaps, but she did remember the little business deal from which a brass replica miners' lamp now hung on offer for sale in the window of her shop. The man had offered her the lamp eight days earlier, on Saturday 14 January – just three days after Renton's murder. She had shown the usual professional lack of interest and eventually, after haggling, had given him £8 for it.

As soon as Mrs McDermott telephoned the information, John Irving, Senior Fingerprint Officer of New Scotland Yard, went to the 'San Fairy Anne' to inspect the lamp, whilst officers from Lancashire hovered hopefully in the vicinity.

At first Irving's efforts were disappointing. There were fingerprints on the lamp, but even without careful comparison he knew they did not match any marks previously found. The situation was one of anticlimax until, on chatting with Mrs McDermott, Irving learned a very interesting fact. During his haggling over price, the man had dismantled the lamp to show its workings and had then reassembled it. Irving dismantled it too – and on the inner glass surface he found finger impressions which did indeed match those found in the bungalow and in the Ford Sierra car.

Fingerprints, it must be said, are of little use in themselves until matched with the person who made them. In a famous northern case some years earlier, matching fingerprints had been found at some fifty cases of burglary, but those crimes were not solved until the man who had made them came into police custody for another reason.

Norman Finnerty found himself facing a similar situation. The prints from the lamp were checked against the 325,000 sets on file at the Lancashire Fingerprint Bureau and against the 3½ *million* on the Police National Computer. None matched.

In something like desperation he now began enquiries at other bureaux where there might be prints not yet included in the computer bank. Eight officers searched manually through another 3,500 sets of prints before they came upon the right set and were able to put a name to the wanted man.

He was Malcolm Stuart Roberts, born in Leeds on 24 March 1953. So far – so good. But where was Roberts to be found? And what was known about him?

His only previous convictions were for minor thefts committed sixteen years earlier, when he was a 'juvenile'. The offences were of a sort that might have been dealt with by a summons, in which case his fingerprints would not have been taken. But some officer had decided to take them.

After an unhappy childhood (no details are on record), Roberts was taken into care at the age of five, and until the age of fifteen he lived in a children's home in Yorkshire. (Renton too, it will be recalled, had spent his early youth in a children's home, but there was a gap of many years between his experience and Roberts', and it is unlikely that any comparison could usefully be drawn.) So much was already on record in Leeds; the rest was not discovered until later, but for convenience it can be summarized here. Roberts moved about the country extensively, working as a casual labourer on building sites and at engineering works, particularly in the London area and in Scotland. In 1972, whilst in London, he met and quite soon married Mary Roberts (née Sterling), born on 23 December 1955 at Broxburn, who had been working in London as a mother's help. After their marriage they went to Scotland and set up home at 29 Calderhall Avenue, East Calder, where in due course a son and a daughter were born to them. Some time later Roberts drifted back alone to London, where he lived in various hostels and lodgings.

The hunt for Roberts was first priority, and no effort was spared to find him. It was not the Lancashire Police, or indeed the Metropolitan Police, who eventually turned up a London address. The information came from the No. 1 Regional Criminal Intelligence Office in Manchester. Roberts, they reported, was thought to live in lodgings at 3 Willis House, Poplar High Street, with a man called David Duncan Howe.

It was enough. Roberts was found there on the evening of Friday 27 January, and Detective Chief Inspector John Park Howarth, of Lancashire, arrested him. At that time Roberts denied all knowledge of the crime.

Meanwhile, many miles away, officers of the Scottish Regional Crime Squad, based on Edinburgh, were working hard on behalf of the Lancashire Police. Working from Roberts' home address in East Calder and through other family connections, Detective Chief Inspector John Gordon Alston recovered the rest of the property, including the television set and the video-recorder. These were carefully examined and, as a further useful link, Roberts' fingerprints were found on them.

Back in London the police had discovered another useful and

important ally in the person of David Duncan Howe, the man with whom Roberts had been living when arrested. Howe, an unemployed man aged twenty-two, made a series of statements, some of them very productive and all damning.

Roberts, he said, had gone on 10 January to the London Armoury, a shop in Commercial Road, London. There he had purchased a bayonet. The sale, at least, could be verified, and though Roberts never admitted this, there seems no doubt that the bayonet was the murder weapon. On the same day, Roberts left Howe's house saying he meant to travel north. He took with him from the house a wooden rolling-pin. Was this the 'blunt instrument'?

Though it was suggested to him, Howe denied having accompanied Roberts on the journey north; he also denied ever having visited Charnock Richard or met Eric Renton, and no evidence was ever found to prove otherwise.

But he did go to Dagenham with Roberts to help him get rid of the Ford Sierra car – and he did help him dispose of certain other items. He was with Roberts when he sold the miners' safety lamp at 'San Fairy Anne', and later he went with him to a quiet stretch of the Regent's Canal at Limehouse, into which Roberts threw the bayonet and the bunch of keys from the Ford Sierra. He went with the police and pointed out the spot where this had happened.

There had, Howe insisted, been bloodstains on the bayonet. Roberts, he said, had mentioned having a previous contact with Eric Renton, had mentioned the bungalow and had referred to a floor safe fitted in the bungalow. There was indeed a floor safe which the police knew about. It had not been interfered with as far as was known, but its very presence gave some credence to what Howe was telling them.

Moreover, Roberts had done one more significant thing, according to Howe. After disposing of the various items, he had gone back to the house, stripped off his clothing, cut the garments to shreds with a Stanley knife, then placed them in a bin-bag which he threw into a rubbish skip outside the house.

Even though Roberts later admitted to the police that he had got rid of his clothing in the way described, the clothing was never found. It would have been taken, it seems, to the Isle of Dogs and there buried on a vast tip, along with tons and tons of other

London rubbish.

But the bayonet and the keys: once again the Metropolitan Police gave practical assistance to the enquiry. Their Underwater Search Unit found first the bayonet and later – though only after a section of the canal had been drained – the bunch of keys.

Roberts began by denying everything that Howe had said. He never did agree the whole of it but some things he had to accept – including his disposal of the bayonet and keys. And eventually he made a confession which must have been at least partly true.

According to Roberts, he had met Renton on only one occasion. He had been hitch-hiking along the M6 motorway, and Renton had approached him at a service area. Renton had invited him home, ostensibly for a meal, but at the bungalow he had begun to make indecent proposals, and in disgust Roberts had stabbed him. He could not remember, he said, which weapon he had used, but he thought it was a kitchen knife taken from the sink. Roberts had then stolen the property 'as an afterthought' and driven off in Renton's car, later to abandon it at Dagenham.

In some respects the story told by Roberts was not in accord with the known facts. In particular he stated that Renton had been naked when he stabbed him. True, the body had been naked when found, but considerable blood-staining had been noticed on the collar areas of the victim's coat, shirt and pullover. Almost certainly he had been wearing those items when stabbed, and Roberts had stripped off his clothing at a later time.

But what Roberts had admitted was more than sufficient for the purpose, and in due course he was charged with murdering Eric Renton on or about 10 January 1984. In reply he wrote: 'I DID KILL THE MAN ON 11-1-84 AND I DID NOT MEAN IT.'

After being committed from Chorley Magistrates' Court on 10 April, he appeared at Preston Crown Court on 29 October. Mrs Grindrod and Mr K. Levan prosecuted on behalf of the Attorney General. A plea of 'Not Guilty' was entered, and the tenor of the defence, implicit at all stages of a week-long battle, was that, if Roberts had done the deed at all, he had done it only under extreme provocation.

But the evidence against him was overwhelming, and at the

close of the evidence and submissions the jury found him guilty as charged by unanimous decision.

He was sentenced to life imprisonment.

The miners' lamp had played its part – but, as the police in Lancashire will tell you, if anyone deserves plaudits it is the unknown policeman who, at Driffield in 1969, decided to take the fingerprints of a juvenile thief, Malcolm Stuart Roberts.

He had not been fingerprinted before or since – until his arrest for murder.

3 Circumstantial Evidence, Accrington 1896

The person who first cries 'Murder!' is himself a suspect. And rightly so. After all, by his own admission he has some knowledge of the crime. Such suspicion lies lightly, however, and is often dispelled early, when the police can eliminate the informant from their list.

But there are exceptions – and a notable example is a shocking case of murder which occurred at Accrington, in Lancashire, just before the turn of the century.

Christopher Hindle was 'a mere child of fifteen' when, on Wednesday 8 July 1896, his trial for murder opened at the Lancaster Assizes before Mr Justice Cave.

He was accused of killing Sarah Coates, aged sixty-one, his employer's wife.

Hindle was born at Accrington on 28 February 1881 and lived with his parents at 2 Chapel Street, Accrington. He attended St Peter's Day School and St Mary's School in the town until the age of fourteen. He reached all required standards.

After leaving school he worked for several short periods as a shop assistant and a telegraph boy until, in January 1896, he was apprenticed to John Coates, cabinet-maker and funeral undertaker. Coates had a workshop in Bridge Street and lived with his wife and son, Thomas, at the combined house and shop, 3 Warner Street, Accrington.

Shortly after 9 a.m. on Tuesday 9 June 1896, Coates left home and went to his workshop, leaving his wife busy with housework. His apprentice, Hindle, was at the workshop when he arrived, as was Thomas Coates. Hindle, he learned, had been seriously late for work – 2½ hours late. It might have been expected that Coates would chastise him but, if he did, the point was never mentioned by any party. What *is* known is that Coates sent Hindle off on a double errand, first to call at the shop of Edward Morris, wood-carver, 13 Lamonious Street, to enquire if there was 'anything ready', and then to the shop in Warner Street, where he was to dust the furniture.

Hindle carried out the first part. He carried some wooden trusses from Morris's shop back to the workshop. Then he went to Warner Street where, according to his own uncorroborated word, he began the second part of the task.

Sometime after 10 a.m. that day (accounts vary as to the precise time) Hindle was seen at the mouth of a closed entry alongside the shop. He was in his shirtsleeves, and there was blood on his hands. He said, 'It's a murder,' or, 'There's murder.'

Warner Street was fairly busy at the time. Benjamin Simpson, a greengrocer, was close by with his horse and cart; Zachariah Barnes, a draper, and Frederick Eltoft, a boot- and shoe-maker, were passing by. All three heard Hindle say something about murder. However, Mrs Sarah Eidsforth and another lady named Smith were making purchases from the greengrocer's cart, and they did not hear anyone say anything. Nor did two workmen standing on a scaffolding at the nearby White Lion Inn. William Riley, landlord of the White Lion, heard nothing from Hindle, though he was standing with his back to Coates' shop. Later on, Hindle went past him at a run.

Some heard – and some did not. And those who heard described Hindle's words as 'spoken, not shouted'. These circumstances, taken with discrepancies in the story he later told, would count heavily against Hindle at his trial.

After making his announcement Hindle went to the workshop in Bridge Street, confronted Coates senior and Coates junior and said, 'Mrs Coates is murdered.' John Coates said, 'Nothing of the sort,' but Hindle said, 'Look at my arms,' and showed him a number of cuts on his right arm.

Thomas Coates hurried home and ran upstairs to his parents' bedroom. He found his mother lying on the floor with her feet under the bed and her head against the wall. She was bleeding badly from the neck. He ran to ask a neighbour to send for a doctor, then went back to his mother and tried to staunch the bleeding, using towels. Meantime Hindle had gone to the surgery of Dr J.S. Clayton. He told the doctor, 'There's a murder at Coates' in Warner Street.'

Dr Clayton went with Hindle to the shop. On the way they met Police Constable Thomas Andrews who had been summoned by the greengrocer, Benjamin Simpson.

Mrs Coates was still alive when Dr Clayton went into the bedroom. She was lying in a pool of blood that extended to the door and was running down the stairs. He removed two towels and saw a wound on the right side of her neck some 3½ inches long. The wound was not bleeding then. Her face was livid, and her lips were blue. There was a silk scarf tied round her neck which was not at the time tight but appeared to have been pulled tight earlier. She was semi-conscious and muttering. He asked her who had done this to her and heard her say, 'Nobody' and 'Turn me over', both repeated several times.

He was joined by Dr Monaghan, Medical Officer of Health for Accrington, and together they treated the woman as best they could, but she died within a few minutes.

Dr Clayton then turned his attention to Hindle's injured right arm. There were numerous cuts, none of them serious. He had blood on his left hand, but this he said was from the right arm. He had received the cuts, he said, in grappling with the man who had attacked Mrs Coates. PC Andrews let him wash the blood off his hands and then applied wet bandages to the cuts. While this was going on, Hindle told the story that, with minor variations, he would always insist was true.

He had been in the shop, dusting the furniture as John Coates had directed. Mrs Coates had been ironing in another room, but she had heard a noise in a bedroom and had gone to investigate. A short time later, Hindle heard a scream and sounds of a struggle coming from above. He rushed upstairs and in the middle bedroom, near the door, saw Mrs Coates struggling with a strange man. The man had a knife in his hand, and there was a gash in Mrs Coates' neck. Hindle got hold of the man by his coat-tails and tried to pull him off, but the man turned on him and struck him several times with the knife, injuring his right arm. The man then broke away, ran down a rear flight of stairs into the back yard and escaped by climbing over the gate into Back Warner Street. Hindle followed him over the gate, screaming 'Murder! Murder!' and ran after him. He followed the man along a back entry into Bank Street and kept him in sight as far as the Wesley Church clock, where he lost sight of him. Hindle then made his way back to the shop and subsequently made his announcement to passers-by in Warner Street.

About this time there seems to have been a lapse of attention by the police. Agnes Clayton, a widow, of 15 Warner Street, had come into the bedroom, having been summoned by John Coates. Mrs Clayton found a folding pocket-knife lying open about a yard from Mrs Coates' body. She handed it to the police *after first rinsing it in the wash-basin.*

Mrs Clayton made another contribution to the affair. She said to Hindle, 'Why didn't you go to the door and scream "Murder!"?' He said, 'I did, but there was nobody about.'

Other police officers had by then reached the scene and listened to the boy. His story found credence with them, at least for a time. Inspector Sinclair asked Hindle to describe the man he had seen, and Hindle said he was about twenty-eight or thirty years old, five feet eight inches tall, with a dark moustache. He was dressed in a navy blue suit with a low waistcoat, a brown cap and a blue tie. And the boy added, 'I can tell him again if I see him. May I go to the railway station and look out for him?' The inspector sent Hindle to Accrington railway station, accompanied by PC Cameron. Sinclair then went to the police station, where he circulated the description to adjoining police areas and sent plain-clothes officers into the town to look for the man.

But belief in the story was short-lived. Twenty minutes later Inspector Sinclair went back to the murder scene and began to interview witnesses. He and Sergeant Bale examined certain blood-drop trails at the foot of the stairs and in the kitchen. One trail led out into the yard, across a corner of the yard and along the covered passage into Warner Street. There was no blood anywhere near the back yard gate, on the gate or on the adjoining wall. Soon afterwards he was on his way to the railway station to speak to Hindle again.

Hindle had spent some time on the platform with PC Cameron and had scrutinized passengers boarding and alighting from two trains. He had seen and rejected one possible suspect. The conversation (lapsing briefly into dialect) had gone thus.

PC Cameron: 'Sithee. Yon's him.'

Hindle: 'Nay, yon's not him. He's too owd, is yon. It were a reet young un, seventeen or eighteen, wi' a big black moustache. Reet thin and tall.'

Taking this at face value, Hindle's 'strange man' had been rejuvenated by some ten years since his story at the house.

When Inspector Sinclair reached the railway station, he found Cameron alone, Hindle having left. He hurried after him and caught up with him in Warner Street. They met Dr Monaghan, and all three went back to the house and upstairs.

'Now just show me the exact position this man was in when you saw him,' the inspector said.

Once again Hindle went through his story, and the inspector checked it, detail by detail. The story itself was much as before, but by now the inspector was able to compare it with statements from witnesses and with physical details from his examination of the scene. He decided to take Hindle to the police station and detain him, ' ...to verify his statement, which gave rise to some suspicion'.

On the following afternoon – Wednesday 10 June – Hindle was taken from the police station to the court room, where an inquest into Mrs Coates' death was to be held before a jury by coroner H.S. Robinson. Hindle had not at that stage been charged but was still 'detained'. The Chief Constable and Inspector Sinclair watched the proceedings, and Hindle was represented by Mr Withers of Messrs Withers & Hargreaves, solicitors. The inquest was a lengthy affair in the circumstances: a trial in itself. During it, the jury and officials visited the scene of the crime because, as the coroner put it, 'It is a mixed up sort of business inasmuch as there is a great deal of up and down stairs and a great many rooms referred to.'

Hindle sat in the defendant's box flanked by a policeman and listened as a number of witnesses gave their evidence.

John Coates recounted his part of the story, then for the first time introduced a new aspect: 'I missed a threepenny bit a few weeks since but I could not tell who had taken it. I have missed money on two or three occasions, once five shillings, another time eight shillings, all from the same drawer.' The implications of this evidence were obvious, but the point was not pursued at that time.

Next came his son, Thomas Coates, who described finding his mother injured. Shown the knife found near the body, he said, 'This is my property. I left it on the window-bottom of my bedroom.' He demonstrated a peculiarity about the knife, a securing clasp at one end which would make it difficult to open for someone not familiar with it. He had never shown the knife to Hindle, who had never handled it as far as he knew.

Nothing further was said about this, but it must have made Hindle's account seem a little less likely. If the knife was the murder weapon – and later medical evidence suggested it was – how could a 'strange man' have found it? Opened it? Used it?

Thomas Coates went on to confirm his father's story about missing money. He described putting the five shillings and the eight shillings in a drawer from which the sums were later missed.

All the witnesses who had been in Warner Street or nearby when Hindle had emerged, saying, 'It's a murder' or words to that effect, were called to describe the incident. Mrs Sarah Eidsforth of 6 Warner Street, directly opposite Coates' shop, said she had been standing near her door and had seen Hindle come out of Coates' shop and run into the entry, 'as though someone was chasing him'. Her attention had been drawn to this because he slammed the door 'hard enough to have broken the glass'. She had been watching the street for some time before that, waiting for the greengrocer's cart, and was certain no one else had come out of the entry. There was no suggestion then of shouts of 'Murder!'. She heard about it only later, after shopping at Simpson's cart.

Benjamin Simpson spoke of hawking vegetables in Warner Street. He saw Hindle, whom he knew, standing near the covered entry beside Coates' shop. He heard Hindle say, 'There's a murder', but the boy was not looking at him and he thought nothing of it. Hindle said the words – he didn't shout them. He then went away down Warner Street. He walked. He didn't run. Later, when the murder was discovered, he went for the police.

Other witnesses who might have been expected to have seen the 'strange man' running from the rear of the shop stated they had seen no such thing. Ellen Bradley's house, 64 Abbey Street, adjoined the rear of Coates' shop, and the backs of the buildings opened into the same yard. She said she knew nothing of the murder until Thomas Coates came to tell her, yet for half an hour before that time she had been ironing in the back room and looking into the yard. She had seen no one in the yard or climbing over the gate. She was certain no one could have done so without her seeing them. William Wilkinson and Alex Forest, both of Blackburn, had been working on scaffolding in the back street only fifteen yards from the Coates' back gate. They had seen no one climb over the gate or the wall, nor had they heard any cry of 'Murder!'. However, both admitted under cross-examination that it was 'possible' they had missed seeing someone.

Rebecca Franks, of 11 Warner Street, was adamant. She had been hanging out washing in Back Warner Street for half an hour. She had talked to the workmen. Apart from them, no one had passed her.

The police evidence threw further doubt on Hindle's story. PC Thomas Andrews said he had examined the back yard gate. 'On top of the gate there are metal spikes,' he said. There were no signs of anyone's having climbed over. The gate was bolted on the inside. Inspector Sinclair described the blood trail he had followed. The trail ended a little way along Warner Street, some spots on the footpath and some in the street. There were no blood marks near the gate or in Back Warner Street. Amongst other things, Sergeant Bale spoke of finding 'threepence in copper, covered with blood' lying in the bedroom near the body.

Dr J.S. Clayton, after describing his actions when first called to the scene, said appearances were against the woman's having taken her own life. The cut on her neck was from right to left. 'From her appearance I concluded she had been strangled. There were marks on her neck as though violent force had been used by hand.' He later examined the cuts on Hindle's arm. They were mostly parallel with each other and in one direction. They were slight – only about two of them through the skin, and one would expect that a man trying to escape would make bigger cuts, but he could not be sure.

Dr Monaghan said that in his opinion, because of the type of throat wound and the strangulation marks, the woman did not take her own life. He had a brisk exchange with Hindle's solicitor.

Withers: 'But cases of suicide by strangulation have occurred in the past.'
Dr Monaghan: 'I am only giving my opinion.'
Withers: 'But doctors differ.'
Dr Monaghan: 'And so do solicitors.'

Dr William Geddie, police surgeon, said that Mrs Coates was dead by the time he reached the house. He had examined the body and later performed a post-mortem examination. Apart from the wound in the throat there were bruises on the neck, some suggesting that fingers had gripped the throat very tightly; also two contused lines round the neck caused by something drawn tight. The neck wound had completely severed the jugular vein. He did not think the injuries could have been self-inflicted.

'My opinion,' Dr Geddie told the coroner, 'is that the woman was attacked twice. She was first strangled almost to unconsciousness, partly by the scarf and partly by hand, and then her throat was cut. She was probably gripped by a left hand: the thumb mark is on the right and the finger marks on the left. The cut suggests the knife was plunged in the right side of the neck, then drawn out at the left side.' Shown the pocket-knife, he added, 'It would inflict such a wound.'

The question if Hindle was left-handed was raised twice, with different witnesses, by the coroner and by a member of the jury, but was never satisfactorily answered.

Respecting the cuts on Hindle's arm, Dr Geddie said: 'I found two cuts through the skin and seventeen scratches – I can't call them anything else. They were all transverse across the arm in one direction. I asked the boy to describe how the marks on his arm were caused. He said he struggled with the man for five minutes. The man caught hold of his wrist and struck him repeatedly with the knife. I do not think they could have been caused the way he described.' And then he added a few words which seem to crystallize what everyone present must have been wondering: 'His wounds might have been self-inflicted.'

Recalled to the stand, Inspector Sinclair said there were no signs of a struggle in the bedroom. There were no blood drops down the stairs, only at the bottom.

At the conclusion of a lengthy summing-up, the coroner told the jury: 'I can see only one verdict – and that is a verdict of murder. If you cannot judge who the person responsible was, you should return a verdict against some person unknown. If you think there is a prima facie case against anyone – I do not say a conclusive case – it is your duty to return a verdict of murder against that person and leave it to another jury to decide.'

After retiring for a little over an hour, the jury returned and the foreman, Councillor Thomas Broughton, announced:

'The unanimous verdict of the jury is that Sarah Coates has been wilfully murdered and that there is strong prima facie evidence against Christopher Hindle ...'

'Then there is a verdict of wilful murder against Christopher Hindle,' the coroner said. He formally committed Hindle to stand trial at the next assizes for the county.

Immediately after the inquest, Inspector Sinclair cautioned Hindle and charged him with the murder of Sarah Coates. Hindle made no reply to the charge.

Among other newspapers, the Accrington *Gazette* carried a report of the inquest, and two unrelated items on the same page give a flavour of the times. First, the commercial:

A LETTER FROM BACUP

I take this method of expressing my gratitude for all that 'Perry Davis' Pain Killer,' has done for me. I had not felt myself for months. My appetite was gone and I suffered constantly from indigestion. It was a rare thing for me to take a hearty meal. 'Perry Davis' Pain Killer,' was recommended to me by a friend, and after I had taken it according to directions for one week, my appetite improved, and my friends say they never saw me looking better and in such good spirits. The pain I always had after eating has not troubled me for some time, and I now consider myself a cured man, and can cheerfully recommend, 'Perry Davis' Pain Killer,' to anyone who is similarly afflicted. Yours very truly, Thomas Gavin. (Address supplied.)

Perry Davis' Pain Killer is sold by all chemists and medicine dealers in bottles at 1s 9d and 3s 6d. The new 1s 9d size contains over twice the quantity of the old 1s 1½d size – British depot, 46, Holborn Viaduct, London, E.C.

And a little lower down:

The execution of Fowler, Milsom and Seaman, the two first named for the Muswell Hill murder and robbery, and the third for the double murder in Whitechapel, took place on Tuesday morning, in Newgate Prison, London, and passed off without a hitch. [Pun?] Milsom was pinioned in a separate room from the others. There was no scene between him and Fowler. All three walked quietly and firmly to the drop, and each met his fate with fortitude.

Hindle made a brief appearance at Accrington Borough Police Court on Thursday 11 June, and public interest had by then caused such crowds to gather that the police had to regulate admission. The charge was outlined but no evidence offered, and he was remanded in custody for seven days, to enable depositions from the inquest to be studied by the Public Prosecutor.

The main police court hearing took place on Friday 19 June and Monday 21 June 1896. Mr Withers again stood for Hindle. The Town Clerk, Mr Aitken, prosecuted on behalf of the Public Prosecutor.

The court was crowded as before with people anxious to gain a glimpse of the prisoner. Hindle is said to have appeared 'pale, but self-possessed'.

Once more the many witnesses were called to give their evidence and, though a few additional facts emerged, the hearing was substantially a repeat of the inquest. There were some sharp interventions by Withers, a few of which might be mentioned.

During his opening address, Aitken said, '... the boy had been suspected of stealing money ...'

That statement brought Withers to his feet, but Aitken

countered his objection by saying he was not stating anything but what he would support by evidence.

Withers: 'We are not in the Coroner's Court now, but in the Magistrates' Court.'
Aitken: 'I am aware of that.'

He went on to allege that during a search of the shop the police had found a sum of money – £1.5s.6d – hidden under a shelf, that there were bloodstains near where the money was found and that more bloodstained money – the three single penny pieces – had been found close to the murdered woman.

Sensing the prosecution line, this clearly was the best motive they could ascribe to the killing: that Mrs Coates had caught Hindle in the act of stealing, that he had been in possession of the pocket-knife from the adjoining bedroom and that he had killed her in order to escape detection. Though there was no direct evidence of this, there was a strong chain of circumstances that supported the theory.

Police Constable Dobie and Detective Sergeant Garvey spoke of searching the shop and finding the hidden money. The sum was made up of silver coins in various denominations. There were bloodstains near it. The search had taken place on Saturday 13 June.

Withers: 'That was four days after the murder.'
Sergeant Garvey: 'We would have searched earlier but did not wish to disturb the family whilst the corpse was in the house.'
Withers: 'The corpse was at the mortuary on Tuesday and Wednesday.'
Sergeant Garvey: 'I was busy with the inquest on those days.'

Cross-examining Inspector Sinclair, Withers pointed out that the lad had been detained for thirty-six hours before he was charged, and he asked the inspector: 'Were you awaiting the verdict of the coroner's jury?'

Inspector: 'No.'

Withers:	'The lad would not have been charged if the verdict had gone the other way.'
Inspector:	'He would have been charged.'
Withers:	'Is it the usual practice of the Accrington police to detain people for that length of time before charging them?'
Inspector:	'No.'

Dr Monaghan said that with Inspector Sinclair he had examined Hindle's arm in Broughton's cloggers' shop.

Withers:	'What Broughton was that?'
Dr Monaghan:	'Councillor Broughton.'
Withers:	'It was the Mr Broughton who was foreman of the Coroner's jury, was it?'
Dr Monaghan:	'Yes.'
Withers:	'Indeed!'

During his evidence, Dr Geddie, police surgeon, referred to Hindle's injuries, which he said he thought were self-inflicted. He had taken a photograph of the arm, which he produced. Withers had objected to the admission in evidence of various things, and now he objected to the photograph.

'It seems to me to be a most extraordinary procedure,' he said. 'The police had a young boy in custody. They did not charge him with anything for thirty-six hours, and without having his parents there or anything they took a photograph of him …'

Aitken countered by saying that the photograph was as much in favour of the boy as against him, and if it was out of order, the judge at the assizes would rule it so.

G.S. Haywood, architect, produced plans of the Warner Street premises, and Herbert Metcalf, photographer, produced photographs of the front and rear.

Sergeant Bale produced the articles he had found on searching the prisoner. These were a watch chain, two watch keys, a watch and chain, a cigar case, two handkerchiefs, a farthing and an apron bearing a stain which he thought was blood.

At the close of the prosecution case Withers announced that the defence would be reserved.

Hindle was ordered to stand while the charge was read out to him. After he had been warned that he was not obliged to say anything in reply unless he wished, he said: 'I am innocent. That man did it.'

He was then committed for trial.

The assize hearing opened on Wednesday 8 July within the grim walls of Lancaster Castle. Mr Justice Cave took his seat, flanked by the High Sheriff of the county and other notable persons. Mr McKeand and Mr Ambrose Jones appeared to prosecute, and Mr Shee QC and Mr D'Arcy represented Hindle. When he stood in the dock, only the top of Hindle's head protruded over the rail. When the indictment was read to him, he replied in a firm voice, 'Not guilty.'

The jury was empanelled, the opening speech made, then one by one the witnesses were called to give evidence, most of them for the third time. There was little new in what they said, though Thomas Coates cleared up a detail.

His mother, he told the court, had been in the habit of wearing a silk scarf like the one found on her body. His father supported this but said he was not sure whether the one found was his wife's or not. Most probably, it was.

The judge and the jury examined the 'peculiar' knife.

All the witnesses were cross-examined by Shee but, that apart, no evidence was called for the defence.

'For Heaven's sake,' McKeand said in his closing remarks to the jury, 'give the lad the benefit of the doubt if you have any, but I submit that there is none: that the whole of Hindle's actions point to his guilt: that, impelled by greed, he seized Mrs Coates, a helpless old woman, completed his deed on her by cutting her throat and then invented the story of a strange man and tried to add to its probability by cutting his own arm. There is not a jot of corroboration that Hindle raised any alarm and pursued the man …'

Afterwards, at Shee's request, Mrs Hindle was called to speak to her son's character. She said he was a good, honest, straightforward boy, most kind and affectionate.

'The boy's age is a material matter,' Shee submitted when his turn came. 'The prosecution say he told lies, but it is one thing to tell a lie and another thing to commit murder.'

He went on to suggest that the real murderer had hidden

himself until the excitement was over, that Hindle was a brave boy who had tried to hold the murderer and that, far from proving his guilt as the prosecution alleged, Hindle's actions went to show that he was innocent. The contradictions in Hindle's statement, which the prosecution said were irreconcilable, might be reconciled by the desire of the police to harmonize them with a theory they had formed. Greed had been suggested as a motive, but it was much more likely that Mrs Coates had hidden the sum of money than that Hindle had done so. To sug-suggest that Hindle would injure himself in order to avert suspicion was contrary to human nature. If it were all true, and if after that Hindle faced the world, then he had a power of resolution and nerve such as was not to be found except in men of rank villainy. Mrs Coates, when asked who had done it, said, 'Nobody.' That alone ought to entitle the lad to a verdict of acquittal.

The defence offered many more, similar suggestions.

In closing, Shee said the police ought to have circulated the description Hindle gave them (they had, according to earlier evidence) but they were wedded to a preconceived theory and sought – honestly, he admitted – to square the facts with their theory of the crime. He invited the jury to acquit the lad.

Mr Justice Cave then summed up.

'Without doubt,' he said, 'Mrs Coates was murdered, and the question you have to decide is whether Hindle or an unknown man was the murderer. If Hindle's tale is true, it was the unknown man who committed the murder. If it is untrue, then the inference is almost irresistible that Hindle was the criminal.'

What earthly reason had the strange man to murder Mrs Coates, he wondered, and why did he start on the expedition without a knife to do the deed? He went on to review the case at length – and in such a way that it could be said he favoured a finding of guilt. The jury certainly thought so, or at any rate that was the way their own minds were directed. After a comparatively short retirement they returned to announce that they found Hindle guilty as charged.

In those days, on such a verdict, the only possible sentence was death – and Mr Justice Cave so sentenced him.

Hindle was not, however, to hang. On Thursday 23 July intimation was received from the Home Office that the sentence had been commuted to one of penal servitude for life.

4 Blood on the Sand, St Annes-on-Sea 1919

'Stab wounds about the head, neck and body, inflicted with some instrument.'

So declared the first report describing injuries to a young woman whose body was found on the sand-hills at St Annes-on-Sea, early on Wednesday 24 December 1919 – the morning of Christmas Eve.

In fact, those stab wounds were bullet holes, and the 'instrument' was a Webley revolver. Three bullets had passed through her body, but a fourth, fired into her thigh, was still present in the wound, giving the lie to the earlier conclusion that she had been stabbed. An impacted wound on top of her head had been caused by a blow from the butt of the same revolver.

The likeliest scenario – put forward at the trial by police surgeon Dr A.C. Elliott of St Annes – was that the woman had first been clubbed with the revolver, then, whilst she lay prone and slightly on her side, four shots had been fired into her body. A second bullet was found a few days later, buried in the sand where her head had lain. The other two were never found.

Of the four main wounds, one was clearly the cause of death. The bullet had entered behind her head and exited under her chin, severing both spine and carotid artery in its course, and death must have been instantaneous.

The St Annes sand-hills occupy a 1¼ mile strip of the Fylde coast of Lancashire, beginning north of the town and ending at the Blackpool boundary, and separating Clifton Drive North – the main route into Blackpool – from the sea. Standing above normal high-water mark, they are a more or less permanent feature, changing shape with the vagaries of weather but affected more by wind than by sea.

Lying in a deep hollow about forty yards above high-water mark and 150 yards from the tram track on Clifton Drive North, the body was well hidden from both sides. It could not have been seen by anyone passing beyond the nearest dunes, but Edward Gillett, a local farmer, was a beachcomber, and when he went out on the morning of 24 December, he was looking for anything he could find. Curiosity took him to within three or four yards of the body, and there the sight of blood stayed him. He withdrew and hurried to the nearby Manchester Children's Home, where he telephoned the police at St Annes.

Police Constables Dixon and Moran went to the scene. They noted that the woman's legs were crossed and that a fur muff lay between her thighs. Her head was lying on two large, flat stones which were heavily drenched with blood. Her skirt and combinations were rucked. Scattered about the body were her hat, tightly rolled umbrella, gloves and handbag. The handbag was lying open at her feet, and among its contents were a gold-mounted cigarette-holder engraved with the initials K.E.B. and F.R.H., a metal case of 'lip carmine', a bank book, two rings, some cash and a number of letters. The cash and rings seemed to rule out robbery as the motive. The letters were written in endearing terms, some signed by 'Tom', others by 'Eric'. The contents of the handbag quickly led to the identification of the woman as Mrs Kathleen Harriet Elsie Breaks of Bradford, Yorkshire.

Among the police officers early on the scene was Detective Sergeant Edward Brown and, whilst he was helping with the search, his attention was drawn to various footprints in the wet sand. Some were clog marks, evidently made by Farmer Gillett, others the heavy prints of his uniformed colleagues' boots, but two sets of marks interested him a great deal. They showed the tracks of a man and a woman walking abreast towards the spot where the body lay. The twin tracks ended close to the body, and a single track, that of the same man, could be clearly seen leading away from the place. Sergeant Brown followed the single track. It led him for some distance across the dunes until he came to firmer ground and coarse grass where it no longer showed. But he persevered and eventually found the track again on the sea side of the dunes. From there it led him back across the dunes towards Clifton Drive North and, though once more the harder ground thwarted him, he came on the footmarks again some eighty yards along the main road. At that point he found the imprint of a right hand in the sand, apparently caused by someone climbing out of a dune hollow. A short distance further, towards the road, he lost the track completely.

The route Sergeant Brown followed was to prove relevant in several ways. The first occurred the same day, when Thomas Henry Gillett (brother of Edward, the beachcomber) was passing along Clifton Drive North in his horse and cart. He found a left-hand gauntlet glove close to the point where the track had ended. The glove was handed to the police. It was bloodstained.

The police surmised from the outset that the woman must have been killed by someone she knew. How else could she have been lured to such a spot at such a time? The sand-hills had their continual population. On warm summer days bathers and picnickers frequented the hollows between the dunes, and by day and night they were the haunt of lovers. But this was late December, damp, cold and blustery. It had rained heavily overnight. The woman had not been dragged there: no signs of a struggle showed except in the immediate vicinity of the body, so it was likely she had gone there willingly. On that assumption, the answer must lie among her past associations. Part of the hunt switched to Bradford.

Kathleen Harriet Elsie Breaks was born at Tickhill, Doncaster, on 19 August 1894. Her maiden name was Fish. She lived with her mother and two sisters at Ryecroft Farm, Dudley Hill, Bradford – and, if the circumstances of her marriage are any guide, she was both wayward and secretive. The ceremony was performed at North Bierley register office, Bradford, on 1 November 1913, but she returned home immediately afterwards and continued to live as though she were single – her family none the wiser.

Her husband, John Stoddard Breaks, kept a garage at Bridlington and lived at 9 Manor Street, Bridlington. They had met whilst she was on holiday in the town. Some relationship must have existed between them, but they did not live together as man and wife until the end of October 1917, almost four years after their wedding. Even when the secret came out, their marriage was short-lived. After only six months residence at 17 Norman Drive, Bradford, they decided once more to live apart.

They were to meet again only about three times – at Ryecroft Farm – and the last time he saw her alive, so Breaks said, was on 14 October 1919, when they drove to Bingley and back again, before parting as good friends.

Married or not, Kathleen Breaks indulged her liking for seaside holidays. She was a frequent visitor to Blackpool and the Fylde coast, where she lived extravagantly and became known at the best hotels. To use an overworked and often meaningless term, she was 'fond of the company of men', but in Kathleen's case the term had special meaning. The police began to look for men in her life.

As will-o'-the-wisp husband, John Breaks was a natural first suspect, but he was able to account so well for his movements at the time of the murder that the police were soon convinced he had contributed nothing to the case other than his name.

The same was soon established of 'Tom', one of the authors of the letters found on the dead woman. He turned out to be Thomas Thornton of 68 Victoria Road, Saltaire, a manager in the pattern department of a shipping firm at Bradford and a friend of Mrs Breaks 'since a girl'. With commendable frankness he described himself to the police as 'an intimate friend' – with whatever connotations that term might have carried. But Thornton was well away from St Annes at the relevant time and was able to prove it convincingly.

The hunt shifted to 'Eric', the other letter-writer, and he was soon recognized as a more promising suspect. His relationship with Kathleen Breaks had been a passionate one, as can be shown by quoting a few samples from his letters to her. About 9 December he had written: 'My dear, darling Kathleen. You dear, sweet thing. You have written me some lovely letters. I do so miss you, dear. Last night I had to take a hot water bottle to bed to help me along till Christmas ...'

In another letter, dated 18 December:

My dear, darling Kathleen. You have no idea how lonely I feel without you. I arrived back safely but do want you near me. You love me and I love you. I feel that I must always be near you. You are the one and only one to me in this world ...

I don't know how to manage without you. I am so longing for Christmas. I feel that you will never leave me. I am sure we shall never part. You and I will be so happy this Christmas and New Year. I know you will make me happy and I will make you happy.

Fine words. No wonder 'Eric' was popular with women.

Frederick Rothwell Holt, who preferred to be known as Eric – an unusual diminutive of his first name – was born at Bleaklow, near Bury, Lancashire, on 2 November 1888. He had a sister and a younger brother. His mother died, his father re-married and the family came to live at 'Holcombe', 9 Lake Road, Fairhaven, within a couple of miles of the sand-hills.

Holt was educated at a private school in Lytham and afterwards took apprenticeship with an engineering firm in Preston. At the age of twenty-two he joined the Army. The *London Gazette* of 20 January 1911 lists his appointment as a 2nd Lieutenant in the 4th Loyal North Lancashire Regiment on 21 December 1910. He served until 1916, when he was honourably discharged after medical boards.

At the time of the murder he was credited with an annual income of £300, a legacy from his mother, though rumour had it that the sum was much greater. Certainly he had no need to work, and if he needed money, it was because he spent too lavishly.

Holt was a known associate of Mrs Breaks, and police enquiries began to elicit useful evidence of this. They had met some time in 1918, during one of her visits to Blackpool, and the strength of her attraction to him is well illustrated in the many letters that passed between them. As the Attorney General was to remark when Holt came to trial, those letters revealed 'a crescendo of affection which continued for over a year'. They saw each other often, and within a few months he was visiting her regularly at Bradford and had been introduced to her family. He took her to restaurants and theatres. The couple were soon booking hotel rooms as 'Mr and Mrs Holt'. But they did not always pose as married. On one occasion they stayed singly at the Clifton Hotel, Blackpool, and Holt, dressed in his nightclothes, was seen near Mrs Breaks' bedroom by the night porter. He excused the incident by saying he had 'got lost'.

But they did stay several times as man and wife at an apartment house, 55 Drewton Street, Bradford. The proprietor, Eliza Byrom, recalled one visit three months previously, another on 17 December 1919 and a third on 22 December, the day before the murder. After the third night's stay at Drewton Street the couple must have set off from Bradford for their final appointment on the bleak sand-hills at St Annes.

Following his arrest, Holt himself supplied some details of the journey, and parts of his story were borne out by independent witnesses. Miss Eva Fish saw Holt at the Midland railway station in Bradford on 22 December and told him her sister (Kathleen) was waiting outside. Between 3.30 and 4 p.m. on Tuesday 23 December – the day of the murder – Kathleen called at the music shop, 28 Sunbridge Road, Bradford, and spoke to her other sister, Daisy Muriel Fish, who worked there. She told Fish she was on her way to Blackpool, travelling with Holt.

They took the Manchester train from Bradford, then the 5.55 p.m. train from Manchester to Blackpool Central. Holt alighted near his home at Ansdell & Fairhaven station, leaving Kathleen to travel on, unaccompanied, to Blackpool. There was evidence that she arrived there safely. At 7.35 p.m. that day she left her luggage in the cloak-room at Blackpool station and went to the nearby Palatine Hotel, where she booked dinner for one. Before leaving the Palatine Hotel, about 9 p.m., she made some enquiries about the Manchester Children's Home and how best to get there. She was advised to take a tram from near the Central station – and there is little doubt that is what she did. Less than twelve hours later, Farmer Edward Gillett was to stumble on her body.

Much was made at the ensuing trial of the circumstances of Mrs Breaks' last known actions. Where had she meant to spend the night of 23 December? Where, indeed, had she meant to spend Christmas? With Holt's parents perhaps? Till then, she had not been introduced to them. Or was she to go with Holt to some other hotel? No room had been booked for her in Blackpool, Lytham or St Annes. After paying for her dinner at the Palatine Hotel she was left with only 25 shillings cash. And significantly, Holt was discovered to have a woman's nightgown in his possession, whilst Mrs Breaks' luggage, recovered from the cloak-room at the railway station, did not contain a nightgown.

As the police began to assemble these facts, they went in search of Frederick Rothwell Holt.

At 9.50 p.m. on Wednesday 24 December Police Inspector Alexander Marshall saw Holt at the Clifton Arms Hotel, Lytham. He told Holt, 'The superintendent wishes to have an interview with you. Will you accompany me to the police station?' Holt said, 'Yes. Wait until I have finished my coffee.' He was taken to Lytham police station and asked to wait.

At 10.30 p.m. Acting Detective Inspector John Sherlock went to Lytham police station. He informed Holt that enquiries were being made about the finding of the dead body of a woman and asked him to go to St Annes police station. Holt accompanied him and on arrival at St Annes, in the presence of Superintendent Foster and Detective Sergeant Gregson, Inspector Sherlock cautioned Holt and said: 'I want you to clearly understand we are making enquiries respecting the death of Kathleen Elsie Breaks whose dead body was found on the sand-hills this morning.' He showed Holt a travelling-bag, a gauntlet glove and a number of letters, and went on, 'Several of these letters we have reason to believe were written by you, and I now give you the opportunity to account for your whereabouts and movements on the 23 December and today.'

Holt seemed anxious to co-operate.

'I will give you all my movements,' he said, 'for I want to help you all I can.' He described the journey from Bradford and the parting at Fairhaven, then: 'On leaving the station I went into the Fairhaven Hotel and stayed there about twenty minutes or half an hour. I then went for a walk round the lake and on the front, near Lowther Gardens, and then back home. It was early for supper, so I had another walk round the lake, then back home again. I got in the house again about 10.15 p.m.'

Asked if he had seen anyone he knew, he went on: 'I never spoke to anybody after leaving the train, and I did not see Mrs Breaks again. I have been enquiring about her all day. We had to meet at luncheon today at the Clifton Hotel, Blackpool. I went there about 12.15 p.m. but she was not there. I asked the Hall

Porter, John, if she came in to tell her I would be back at one o'clock.'

Reminded about the letters, he said: 'I wrote them to her. While I was in Bradford along with Mrs Breaks I met Daisy Fish, who works at a piano shop in Sunbridge Road. When I arrived in Bradford on Monday the 22nd, about 12.45 p.m., Mrs Breaks met me at the railway station and we stayed together that night at 55 Drewton Street. We have stayed there before.'

The inspector noticed a scratch on Holt's wrist and four scratches on his left cheek. In explanation, Holt offered: 'The scratch on my wrist may have been done by a dog or a cat, and those on my face I have done them with my razor.'

Asked if he was still wearing the same clothes, he said: 'No. I was dressed in a grey suit, a blackish grey overcoat and was wearing leather gloves. As a matter of fact I left them somewhere.' He pointed to the glove on the desk. 'That is one of them. I hadn't the gloves when I got out of the train. The suit is hanging on the back of my bedroom door, and the overcoat on the rail on the landing.'

At that stage, Inspector Sherlock told Holt that they were not satisfied with his story and that he would be detained.

Parts of Holt's account proved to be manifestly untrue. In the course of checking it, Detective Sergeant Brown took a stroll around Fairhaven Lake, Lytham, and found it took him twenty-four minutes. If Holt had done that twice and had also strolled along the front near Lowther Gardens, it would indeed account for much of the vital time. His father was prepared to support his story that he had reached home around 10 p.m., and the alibi was complete.

But there were witnesses who said otherwise.

John Garlick, a tram conductor with the Blackpool, Lytham & St Annes Tramway Company, reported that about 7.25 p.m. on 23 December Holt boarded his tram at Lake Road, Ansdell, paid a threepenny fare and got off near the Manchester Children's Home.

John Mills, a motorman with the same company, saw Holt, whom he knew, waiting at the tram stop at St Annes Road West, St Annes, at 10.26 p.m. on 23 December.

And evidence from other witnesses was to show that in two specific instances Holt had gone to great trouble to throw suspicion away from himself. Herbert Beardsworth, head waiter at the Clifton Hotel, Blackpool, remembered that Holt had come to the hotel about 12.45 p.m. on 24 December, booked lunch for two and asked Beardsworth to 'keep the table'. Holt stayed in the hotel lobby, 'looking upset', until about 1.30 p.m., when he told Beardsworth, 'It's very strange. I will come in myself.' He did not take lunch, however. He told the 'boots', John Reddington, 'If Mrs Breaks comes, I shall be about.' He left the hotel, saying he would return about 5 p.m. He did come back about that time, when he enquired if there were any messages.

In the interval he had sent a message of his own – a reply-paid telegram which he handed in at Blackpool post office at 2.59 p.m. It was addressed to Daisy Fish, Ryecroft Farm, Dudley Hill, Bradford, and it read: 'Wire me Kathleen's address. Hope you and Eva like handkerchiefs. Merry Christmas. Eric.'

Daisy, seriously upset by the recent news of her sister's death, sent the reply: 'Come at once. Bad news concerning Kathleen. Daisy.'

He was playing the innocent man – and Daisy, at least, had fallen for it, as the wording of her reply indicates. Of course, if he genuinely had not known at that time, then he *was* innocent, for, though the news must have been buzzing around Blackpool, it was possible he had not heard it.

The police thought otherwise. On the strength of the evidence they already had, they charged Holt with the wilful murder of Kathleen Harriet Elsie Breaks, reading the chill formula to him at 7.30 a.m. on Christmas Day.

More evidence was soon to be discovered.

Returning to Holt's home, Detective Inspector Sherlock and Detective Sergeant Brown took possession of various items of clothing and personal effects including suits, coats, shoes, socks, handkerchieves, gloves, razors and contraceptives; also a total of sixty-six letters, telegrams and cards and fifty French picture cards of a pornographic nature. This property was delivered to Bernard (later Sir Bernard) Henry Spilsbury, lecturer in pathology at St Bartholomew's Hospital, London, who examined them and gave evidence about them at the trial.

A burberry coat was found to carry stains of blood and spermatozoa in several places, as well as sand and fibres. The shoes were wet and caked with sand. The French picture cards were not considered significant, but it is a wry fact that they went missing during the trial and were never found again.

Also in Holt's room the police found and took possession of a Colt revolver, military issue. This, however, was Holt's Service revolver, had not been recently fired and was found to have no bearing on the murder.

The shoes were obviously important, and elaborate tests were made to compare them with the footmarks found near the body. The shoes worn by the dead woman were similarly dealt with. Each shoe was pressed into the sand near the place where the body had been lying, and the resultant impressions were measured and photographed. Then Detective Sergeant Brown and Inspector Sharman filled boxes with sand, carried them to St Annes police station and made further impressions from the shoes. The impressions were photographed by Ralph Jones, private photographer, of 3a Orchard Road, St Annes. Holt's shoes had been recently soled, and the new sole showed clearly in the tracks made at the scene and the comparison impressions. Finally, plaster casts were made of the impressions – today they are on display in a small museum at the Lancashire Constabulary Training School.

On Sunday 28 December two more pieces of evidence were found and fitted into place. At 10.30 a.m. Jane Elizabeth Maurice of the Ormerod Home, south of the Manchester Home, was walking on the shoreline when she found a right-hand gauntlet glove. She took it to the Home and handed it to a worker there called Will Sharratt, suggesting he might dry it out and use it for his work. Having just read an account of the murder in the *Empire News*, Will Sharratt handed the glove to the police. It proved to be the mirror twin of the glove found earlier, and it too bore stains that were probably of blood.

A few hours later, whilst walking on the foreshore with his friends, a curious schoolboy, Clifford Forsdike, poked a stick into a pile of sand and uncovered a Webley revolver. He took it to St Annes police station and handed it to Inspector Sharman. This was undoubtedly the murder weapon. When broken, the cylinder was seen to contain four empty cartridge cases and two unfired cartridges. Significantly, the spot where the revolver was found lay within half a yard of the track earlier followed by

Sergeant Brown.

The gloves had been bought by Holt at Thompsons' shop, 60 West Crescent, St Annes, on 28 November 1919. Maggie Thompson, daughter of the proprietor, recalled the transaction and identified the gloves. They had cost Holt £1.7s.6d.

The Webley revolver was identified too. It had been sold at Burrows', gunsmiths, 116 Fishergate, Preston, to F.R. Holt, Lieutenant, 4th Loyal North Lancashire Regiment, on 14 August 1914, when that regiment was billeted at the Public Hall in Preston. The revolver was an RIC model (as issued to the Royal Irish Constabulary). Its serial number had been filed off, but Mr Burrows was able to show that, when the handle was unscrewed, the number was repeated on the inside, a fact few people would be aware of. Holt had evidently not been aware of it.

In spite of the evidence ranked against him, Holt continued to deny the murder. At time of charging, when appearing at lower court and all through his trial at assizes, his plea was consistently 'Not guilty'. It has been said in the press that he *never* admitted his guilt. Was that true? It might not have been.

Before the trial, information was received from the brother of a man then serving a sentence at Strangeways Prison, Manchester, to the effect that the prisoner had had a conversation with Holt in which Holt had admitted his guilt. This might have been a false story by a publicity-seeker – they often are – and in any case the information was never given in evidence, on the obvious grounds of inadmissibility. But what does the modern reader think?

'You did her in all right,' the fellow-prisoner is said to have told Holt, who replied: 'They have not proved me guilty yet.'

'But you did the job?'

'Yes. I first hit her, then shot her. Why I did it was because they were all after me for money. They were always after money.'

The weakness in the story is that 'why he did it' was not the reason given here but rather the opposite. *Holt wanted money.* Whilst it was true that in the months prior to December he had signed a series of cheques in Mrs Breaks' favour – one for £100, which was a handsome sum in those days – the real purpose behind those payments had been the financing of an insurance policy of £5,000 on Mrs Breaks' life. As pointed out in an editorial in *The Times*, dated 28 February 1920, this would have been £10,000 if Holt had had his way. It was shown that he had made several attempts to obtain life insurance in higher sums, had told lies in the process and had had his proposals turned down. It would be illegal, he was told, since he had no insurable interest in her, and if – as was proposed – he paid the premiums himself, he could not benefit unless she left him the money in her will.

Eventually, with the assistance of Mrs Breaks herself, he persuaded the Royal London Company to issue a policy on her life for £5,000. Not surprisingly, his next step was to persuade her to make a will in his favour. She needed little persuading. The will was made and she happily visited the offices of Perkins, solicitors, 9 Charles Street, Bradford, in order to sign it before witnesses. Apart from bequests of £100 to her mother and £100 jointly to her sisters, she left 'my wedding ring and the proceeds of my life insurance policy to Frederick Rothwell Holt, free from any trust whatsoever'. Thus, as was pointed out at the trial, by Mrs Breaks' death Holt stood to gain £4,800. As good a motive for murder as there has ever been.

Kathleen Breaks can have seen nothing sinister in it. Their relationship waxed stronger. In one letter to 'Eric, darling', dated 11 December 1919, she excelled herself in terms of affection, calling him 'Face-ache' and 'Whiskery-face' in a context of familiar endearment.

All these things were to count against Holt when his trial took place at Manchester Winter Assizes commencing Monday 20 February 1920. Mr Justice Greer presided. Counsel for the prosecution were the Attorney General (Sir Gordon Hewart), Mr Merriman KC and Mr Jordan, and for Holt, Sir Edward Marshall Hall KC, Mr W. Wingate-Saul KC and Mr McKeever.

As well as his alibi claim, which he continued to pursue in the face of contrary evidence, Holt sought through counsel to establish doubts as to his sanity as a second-string defence. They alleged that when he committed the act he was suffering from delusion and temporary insanity by reason of jealousy. These efforts had begun well before the trial, when solicitors acting for Holt had interviewed Constable Moran and (pensioned) Sergeant Crompton. Whilst their client was detained in police cells, had he not complained to the officers of seeing insects and dogs attacking him? Both men ridiculed the claims.

Nevertheless, in the course of the trial a 'strange' document written by Holt whilst detained at Strangeways Prison was read to the court. It was a long, rambling screed, full of errors, and a few extracts from it may be of interest: 'Dogs. Wednesday. Christmas Day. 25th. Three attempts with dogs at two-hour intervals.'

This was followed with virtually incomprehensible accounts of three separate attacks by dogs coming through the cell window: 'More. Gas. Flies, which did not leave the floor ... Shooting at me in the cell with explosive bullets filled with mercury ... Swarms of aunts [ants] ... Chewed tobacco and dropped it on the floor. Aunts ate it and swelled up ...'

The defence was unsuccessful. After retiring and deliberating for less than an hour, the jury returned to announce a verdict of guilty – and Holt was condemned to death by hanging.

There was, however, an appeal in which fresh evidence was sought to be admitted. This hearing took place on Monday 15 March 1920, before the Court of Criminal Appeal consisting of the Lord Chief Justice (Lord Reading) and Justices Bray and Avory.

The basis of the fresh evidence was a telegram, supported by a longer letter, from a Dr Bernard Day, who had treated Holt on the Malay Peninsula in 1917. The doctor, who had recalled the matter after reading an account of the trial, stated that Holt, then working in Malaya, had come to him suffering from syphilis which had been allowed to proceed for some six weeks before he saw him. He had given Holt certain injections and advised him to continue the treatment for at least two years. Holt was not at that time insane, though '... he is of such abnormal mentality as more easily to *become* insane – did the syphilis affect his brain – than would the average man.'

This evidence and a good deal more was admitted and listened to. Sir Edward Marshall Hall's contention was that the proper verdict in Holt's case should be, 'Guilty, but insane'.

The court gave its verdict, saying that: '... for all these reasons the testimony given today does not really add anything material to what has already been before the jury and upon which the jury found their verdict. There is no ground for impeaching the verdict, and the appeal will be dismissed on all points.'

On hearing the decision, Holt turned sharply and walked from the dock. Sir Edward Marshall Hall, however, is said to have fumed against the hanging of a 'madman'.

In due course Holt was hanged at Strangeways Prison.

A postscript

Twenty-eight years later, in November 1948, a curious correspondence occurred in connection with the case. A letter addressed to the Chief Constable of Lancashire was received from Keystone Pictures Incorporated, 219 East 44th Street, New York. It requested details, pictures etc of the Sand-hills Murder, including reference to the police officers involved in the investigation. This information was required by 'at least two' American detective magazines.

The Chief Constable, W.W. Thornton, was reluctant to grant the request and sought the advice of the Director of Public Prosecutions, Sir Theobald Matthew.

Sir Theobald did not think it was a good idea, and on the strength of that the request was refused.

5   The Revealing Cloak, Hollinwood 1830

Multiple rape, attacks on elderly women and murder are only too common today, and it is fashionable to blame the spread of violent conduct on modern phenomena: television brutality, drugs, the permissive society, lack of parental and school discipline; but lust began with Adam, and murder with his son, and so it has been throughout the life of man.

Irishwoman Mrs Sarah McCrinn, of Bolton, was at least sixty-four years old and possibly older when, on 22 December 1830, more than a hundred and fifty years ago – she was set upon by a gang of young men, raped repeatedly and left dead or dying in a ditch beside the road from Manchester to Oldham.

One remarkable feature of the case is that Mrs McCrinn was attacked miles away from her home. She was *walking* from Bolton, having been invited to spend Christmas with her married daughter, Mrs Bridget Cheetham, and her grandchildren, who lived at Oldham. As can be imagined, transport was hard to come by in those days and travelling on foot an accepted necessity, but bearing in mind the average weather conditions in late December, the absence of made roads as we know them today and the poor lighting, where there was any at all, it must have been a daunting venture, even for a sturdy woman like Mrs McCrinn, to set off alone on a journey of some twenty miles.

She had made her way to the district of Hollinwood, within a few miles of Oldham, when she was set upon, and there, on the following day, a Mr Schofield found her lying dead. Schofield was a surveyor, working in fields in the area, and (somewhat surprisingly in view of the position and state of the body) he did not at first realize that she had met a violent end. The clothing was so disarranged that the body was naked from the waist downwards; there was blood around the mouth, and a scratch above one knee. Her cloak was missing too, though Schofield could not have been aware of that.

Even more surprising was the opinion of Mr Newton, a surgeon called to examine the body and perform a post-mortem examination. Newton found signs of haemorrhaging into the brain tissue, though not very much, and having no reason to suspect murder he concluded she had died of apoplexy and was prepared to record the old woman's death as 'Accidental'. It is easy to be critical and probably unfair. The surgeon did not have at hand the tools of modern investigative medicine, nor was he blessed with hindsight. To be charitable, let us leave it that his findings seem to have lacked perception.

The actual cause of death, though not recorded, is easy to imagine when the facts are known. To be held down and raped successively must have induced shock and may have brought unconsciousness. Had she been found more quickly after the event, Mrs McCrinn might have survived, but she was thrown half-clad into a ditch and remained there all night in conditions that were undoubtedly cold and more than likely freezing. Even an unprofessional hypothesis would suggest that she died from exposure following injury and shock.

What authority existed in 1831 to investigate the murder of Sarah McCrinn? There was no countrywide police force as we know it today. The Metropolitan Police had been founded by Sir Robert Peel only two years before, and the Municipal Corporations Act, requiring boroughs to appoint watch committees, who were in turn to establish local police forces, was not passed until five years later.

Outside London, the preservation of the King's Peace was largely a matter for local arrangement, and because of varying attitudes arrangements varied widely from place to place. The raising of 'hue and cry' had generally fallen into disuse, and men were responsible for the safety of their own goods and lives. Watchmen were appointed in some areas, and from these developed the system of appointing town constables to serve for short periods – usually a year. But the work was not popular. It was in most cases a chore, visited in turn on all suitable citizens, for which no payment was made. Small wonder that well-to-do businessmen objected to a system by which they were obliged to neglect their lucrative trades and go to work as constables – for nothing. Even for only a year, such a duty was bad news. Small wonder, too, that in many places the practice grew of appointing substitute constables and paying them a small wage to take over the stints of more prosperous people. At first, this was a personal arrangement, and some of the most unsuitable men – aged, crippled, lazy, even dishonest – were employed as constables and not once but time after time, as succeeding clients hired their services. The situation was unsatisfactory and could not be allowed to go on. The practice was introduced of the townspeople, as a body, appointing constables and paying them reasonable wages. Better standards were set and the system gradually improved.

Effectively, still, the burghers of a town were the law; and of course there were also Justices of the Peace. The holders of this ancient office had for centuries acted as executive law officers as well as judiciaries. They controlled such watchmen or constables as there were and took personal charge of controlling serious breaches of the peace. Murder was foremost in their jurisdiction. Almost certainly it would have been a local Justice of the Peace who, aided by whatever staff were available, tackled the investigation into Sarah's death.

It is also safe to say that a borough as well established and commercially important as Oldham would have had constables, though whether their patrols extended to Hollinwood is uncertain. There was at least one watchman on duty in the district. Thomas Jones was so appointed for nearby Newton Heath, and he was one of three people able to testify in part to Sarah McCrinn's journey.

About 9 p.m. on Wednesday 22 December 1831 Thomas Jones saw an elderly woman walking along the road in the direction of Oldham. She was small and stocky, and from her speech he judged her to be Irish. He had a short conversation with her and, though he did not ask her name, learned she was making her way to the home of her married daughter in Oldham, where she was to spend Christmas. While these two were talking, they were joined by another man, named Robert Lees, who happened also to be walking in the Oldham direction. Lees said he would walk with the woman and keep her company. When he was later interviewed, Lees said they had walked together for a mile and a half, after which she could no longer keep up with him and he left her behind.

Asked to describe the woman they spoke to, both these men spoke of the long cloak she was wearing.

Between 9 p.m. and 10 p.m. on the same night, a woman knocked at the door of a cottage occupied by Mrs Moon, on the Oldham Road and a little nearer to Oldham. She wanted a drink of water, and Mrs Moon supplied her with it. Mrs Moon's description of the woman tallied with those of Jones and Lees.

There is no doubt the caller was Sarah McCrinn – and Mrs Moon was the last person, apart from her killers, to see her alive.

The fact that these three witnesses were found is a good indication that enquiries were made then much as they would be made today. Following discovery, the body was taken for laying out at Newton church, and the watchman, Thomas Jones, was taken there to see it. He identified it as the body of the woman he had spoken to the previous evening.

His Majesty's Coroner for the district would be informed and an inquest held, though no record of the verdict has been traced.

The news spread wide through the mouths of seekers and gossips alike – and there were public-spirited citizens then, as there are now. A whisper was needed – and it came.

A few days later, by a means unknown, the authorities learned that two local men, Ashton Hutton and William Mellor, had come by a cloak of the type usually worn by women. The cloak was seized and the men were questioned. Since it is not recorded, who can say what explanation the two gave? But soon afterwards the cloak was identified by a neighbour of Mrs McCrinn in Bolton as one she had lent to the old lady for the journey.

The cloak was damning evidence unless possession of it could be explained away. Hutton and Mellor could not manage that. They were arrested and charged with the murder. And yet they were freed shortly afterwards, for reasons that can only be guessed at.

All that is known is that the two men were brought before the magistrates and acquitted. William Mellor played no further part in the matter, but Ashton Hutton began to talk, and since it then became apparent that he knew a great deal about the murder at first hand, the conclusion is irresistible that some sort of deal was struck between Hutton and his captors. Hutton did not quite 'turn King's Evidence'. That term described the case where a criminal confessed and betrayed his accomplices in exchange for his own immunity. Hutton's position was rather that he had witnessed the crime but had played no part in it and was innocent.

He told the following story:

On the evening of the crime he had been drinking at a local beerhouse with a number of other men, among them Robert Chadderton, aged twenty-two, and two brothers, William Worrall, thirty-eight and Ashton Worrall, twenty-five.

They left the beerhouse about 9.30 p.m. and crossed some fields, heading towards the spot where the body was later to be found. They came to a hedge, and from somewhere beyond the hedge Hutton heard voices. Some were deep and obviously male, but he also heard a woman's voice, shrill and anxious, saying, 'Oh! Dear me,' or something like that. Moments later, the woman's voice shouted, 'Murder!' And the call was repeated several times.

Looking over the hedge, Hutton witnessed the combined assault on Sarah McCrinn. He saw three men holding her down and watched as each in turn raped her. He named the three men as Ashton Worrall, William Worrall and Robert Chadderton. He was sure about the first two, not so sure about Chadderton, since he never saw his face. When they had done with her, the three men picked up the woman, who appeared silent and still, and tossed her into the ditch. That done, they walked away in company with Hutton. Ashton Worrall was carrying a bundle under his coat. As they were walking along Oldham Road they met another man. Ashton Worrall took out the bundle, handed it to the newcomer and said, 'Here. Take this and say nothing about it.'

Hutton's story was full of holes such as any child could have crawled through. He went to the place in the company of the other three, so how did it happen that he saw nothing until the attack was in progress? At what point did he separate from the others so that they were beyond a hedge, engaged in their crime, when he got there? Even if he didn't recognize Chadderton taking part in the attack, surely he must have done so afterwards as they were walking away together? What was in the bundle Ashton Worrall carried? Who was the newcomer to whom he subsequently gave it? Not a stranger, surely, since Worrall would scarcely have enjoined a stranger to silence.

Hutton was asked at the trial why he did not go to the aid of the wretched victim. He replied that he would gladly have done so but he was only one against three – and he was afraid of Ashton Worrall.

The truth must lie somewhere beyond the words of Hutton's story. Was he a party to the crime, and should the tally of rapists really have been four – or more? Or was he afraid to take part (his cronies would surely have invited him) and instead took refuge behind the hedge until it was over? And that bundle! Surely it could only have been Sarah's cloak? Hutton himself was later found in possession of the cloak, along with William Mellor. Was Mellor, then, the unnamed man to whom Ashton Worrall handed the bundle with instructions to remain silent?

The final flaw in Hutton's story seems to illustrate the kind of man he must have been. Perhaps he was innocent of the attack, perhaps he would have helped the woman if he could, but he kept his mouth shut for several days and would have continued to do so had he not been arrested. He also kept the cloak, knowing very well where it had come from. So at best Hutton was dishonest. He was almost certainly conscienceless also.

But the story he told was very useful. The brothers Worrall and Robert Chadderton were arrested and charged with rape and murder of Sarah McCrinn. After appearing before the magistrates several times, they were indicted at the Lancaster Spring Assizes on Saturday 12 March 1831. All three pleaded 'Not guilty' to the charges.

In addition to the witnesses already mentioned, several others testified to having heard Sarah's cries of 'Murder!' And a Mr Berry, who had been in the field shortly after the body was found, added another telling detail. He deposed that Ashton Worrall had come into the field and they had had a short conversation. Worrall asked him, 'Is it true they've found a dead woman?' Berry told him it was true and at Worrall's query pointed to the place in the ditch where Sarah had been found. According to Berry, Worrall then remarked: 'Damn it. I wish I'd never had anything to do with her.'

But above all else, Hutton's evidence was the base on which the prosecution case rested. The issue hinged on whether or not the jury believed it.

The only defence offered by the Worralls was denial of the evidence and assertion of complete innocence. Chadderton, however, put up an alibi – and must have done it convincingly, as he was eventually acquitted. Ashton Worrall and William Worrall were not so lucky. The jury found them guilty as charged, without even bothering to retire.

Both the Worralls were then sentenced to death, the execution to take place on the following Wednesday at Lancaster Prison. (Such matters were not long delayed in those days.)

In accordance with common practice before an execution, the convicted men were interviewed by clerics who urged them to confess their sins, but they refused to do so. At 8.30 a.m. on 16 March, observed by a crowd said to number some 3,000, they were brought out pinioned to the scaffold and hanged. Immediately before going to his death, Ashton Worrall is reported to have shouted:

'Lord have mercy on me! I am as innocent as a child.'

6 The Kay's Houses Killers, Wigan 1895

'Kay's Houses', reported the *Wigan Observer* in October 1895, 'have had an unenviable reputation for years.'

That was no libel. The cluster of cottages so named stood in the county area of Lower Ince, close to the boundary with Wigan borough, and if there was trouble in that vicinity, any gambling man would have risked a shilling or two in plumping for Kay's Houses as its source.

Some of the cottages must have housed honest men, but there were many of the other sort. A number of residents had been convicted of theft, burglary and assault, and some of those not convicted were suspected of being active thieves. Good pickings were to be had virtually on the doorstep. A few hundred yards from Kay's Houses, just on the far side of Chapel Lane, Wigan, and protected only by a stone wall and sleeper fence, stood the warehouses and goods sidings of the London & North-Western Railway Company.

During September 1895, and for some weeks before that, there had been frequent raids on the sidings and much property stolen from loaded goods trains temporarily standing there. In the main the offences had been committed at week-ends, in the period between Saturday noon and Monday morning when the goods depot was closed. The company were anxious to put an end to the thefts, and they deployed plain clothes officers at the goods depot each week-end to patrol and keep observations.

A local officer, Detective Constable William Henry Osborne, had often been called on for such duties, but on Sunday 29 September arrangements had been made for outside help. When the 7 p.m. train left Manchester for Wigan, Detective

Sergeant Robert Kidd was on board.

Sergeant Kidd was thirty-seven years old. He lived with his wife and seven young children at 17 Zebra Street, Salford, and was stationed at Manchester, but like all railway policemen he commonly travelled to other towns when help was needed. He knew the goods depot at Wigan and had worked there often before.

The sergeant arrived at Wigan station about 8 p.m. and was met by Detective Osborne. Osborne gave him a cloth cap to wear in place of his normal hat, then the pair set off walking southward beside the main line, making for a part of the sidings where recent thefts had occurred. It was a clear night, and visibility in the moonlight helped them on their way.

They walked in the shadow of a wall that bounded the sidings and, coming to the end of the wall, Osborne, who was leading, held up a hand to halt Kidd and whispered, 'Hush.' Almost immediately he saw a man on hands and knees beside the wall and, thinking it might be a railway employee, said, 'Hello. What do you want?' The man echoed the words, 'What do you want?' Then he shouted, 'Hey up, lads. Have you got it?' and started to run.

Leaving Kidd, Osborne ran after the man. He caught up with him alongside a goods wagon a few yards ahead, but the man had no intention of being taken. They struggled fiercely, falling down several times as they fought. Osborne was kicked many times on the shins and in the groin and also got in a blow or two of his own. They had moved some distance along the siding before he managed to subdue the man. 'When I got him down,' he later told the court, 'I got my knee into him and was shaking his head on the ground.'

Till then, Osborne had seen only one man, but a second man ran round the corner of the wagon and kicked him on the left knee. Having done so, the man stumbled and fell but got up again. Osborne left the first man, who appeared to be exhausted, and grappled with the second man, but at that moment a third man appeared running towards him. The third man was holding his arm high and there was something in his hand – something that glinted brightly in the moonlight, 'like a piece of glass', as Osborne stated later.

Osborne reached for his truncheon but missed the haft and

caught only the leather thong. He swung it flail-like at the approaching man and struck him a blow on the upraised hand. The man was evidently hurt, for he put the hand up to his mouth. By this time Osborne was weary and losing the struggle, and when the two men pulled away from him and took to their heels, he did not follow. He went back to the first man, who was still on the ground but by no means submissive, and kicks and blows were exchanged between them. Osborne tried to hold on to him but could not. The man wrenched the truncheon from Osborne's hand, broke away and ran off towards Kay's Houses.

We have a fairly detailed account of Osborne's actions because he was able to recount it. What had happened in the meantime to Sergeant Kidd remains uncertain and must be pieced together in the light of what was learned from later events.

In the heat of the struggle Osborne had lost contact with Kidd, and now he went in search of him. About that time he heard sounds as of several people jumping into the street from the nearby gas works bridge. He went on and found Kidd in 'number five roadway' between the wall and a line of wagons. Kidd was in a collapsed state, on hands and knees. He turned his head, and Osborne saw blood running down his face. 'I thought he had been kicked,' he said later. 'He spoke to me, saying "Osborne. Is that you? Get me a drink of water." '

Osborne picked Kidd up and began to carry him towards a nearby signal box but fell after a few yards and could not carry him further. He went on alone, alerted the signalman and staff at the main platform, then fainted from his injuries. He recovered sufficiently to gasp out a rather garbled story and was then taken to Wigan Infirmary and detained.

There was some support for Osborne's account of having heard the sound of men jumping over the gas works bridge. A witness was found who had seen three rough-looking men on the bridge about the same time. The witness could not identify any of the men but had heard one of them say what sounded like: 'One of the buggers is dead and the other is left to die.'

Sergeant Kidd was certainly dead when other officers came on the scene. His clothing was badly cut and stained and there was blood on his hands, face and clothing. He had been terribly injured. As medical evidence would show, he had been beaten and stabbed repeatedly with some sharp instrument, probably a knife. There were nine punctured wounds on the head, face and neck, and three of these had penetrated to the blood vessels of the neck. There was a jagged slash across the right cheek, baring the bone. One nostril was almost slit away. There were numerous abrasions on neck, face, left arm and both hands – and the tip of the left index finger had been cut off, showing that very great violence had been used. The three most severe wounds in the neck had been the primary cause of death.

A carefully organized search of the siding revealed signs of a desperate struggle. Large patches of blood were found in several places, suggesting that Kidd had dragged himself for some distance across a railway track. Four cloth caps were found, one of them that loaned to Kidd by Osborne, which was heavily stained with blood. A second cap was Osborne's own. The other two would be wedded to their owners by evidence at a later time.

Loaded wagons standing nearby contained a variety of merchandise, and three of them had been broken into. Three cases of condensed milk were missing, and a bottle of cough lozenges, taken from bulk, was found lying close to one of the wagons. The string on a bale of such bottles had been cut with a sharp knife.

The Railway Police have jurisdiction on all railway property and for some distance beyond, but in serious cases it has always been customary to seek the aid of the police force through whose territory the line passes. Thus the Wigan borough police were informed, and there was some confusion at first, as the scene of the crime was thought to be in the Lancashire County Police area. In fact, it was just within the borough, but such is the co-operation between forces that thereafter the Borough and County Police worked together with railway officers on the case. Superintendent Macintosh, who was in charge at Wigan in the absence of the Chief Constable, Captain Bell, made enquiries, and not surprisingly he began at Kay's Houses and in adjoining Spring View, also known to be inhabited by convicted railway thieves.

It has to be said that in those days things were done without compunction that would cause a public outcry today. During that night and in the course of the next two days, eight men were arrested and charged jointly with the murder, seven of the eight coming from Kay's Houses – yet at Wigan Magistrates' Court on Thursday 3 October no evidence was offered against five of the men and they were discharged.

The eight men originally arrested were: David Millington, Ralph Birchall, James Winstanley, James Wellens, Elijah Winstanley, William Kearsley and William Halliwell, all of Kay's Houses; the odd man out was Richard Pritchard of 25 Grippen's Buildings, Bamfurlong, who was a frequent visitor to Kay's Houses.

Pritchard and the first four listed soon left the court. Elijah Winstanley, William Kearsley and William Halliwell were remanded in custody, charged with murdering Sergeant Kidd and with causing grievous bodily harm to Detective Osborne.

All three men were colliers. Elijah Winstanley was thirty-one years old, Kearsley forty. Halliwell is thought to have been of similar age but it was not given. Indeed, the police seem to have avoided saying overmuch about Halliwell at all stages.

The inquest on Sergeant Kidd was opened on Tuesday 1 October and adjourned after brief evidence. On the same day it was announced that Louis Tussaud was on his way from London to prepare a waxwork effigy of the dead man. Opinions differed as to whether this was proper, but it seems the waxwork was made, using a death-mask moulded from the body, and exhibited in the town.

Two factors were primarily responsible for the selection of Kearsley, Halliwell and Elijah Winstanley as the culprits. The first was that Osborne identified them. All eight arrested men were brought before him at Wigan Infirmary in turn and at different times, each man standing in a line with members of the public in a series of identification parades. He first identified Kearsley as the man who had kicked him on the knee, then Halliwell as the man who had made off with his truncheon, and finally Elijah Winstanley as 'very much like' the man he had seen running towards him with something shiny in his hand.

The second factor was simply that Halliwell had decided to confess. How much information he gave the police cannot be said with certainty, but the story he told when called to give evidence at the preliminary hearing on 10 October was as follows:

On the 29th September I was living at Kay's Houses,

Lower Ince. I have known Elijah Winstanley about three years and Kearsley ever since I can recollect. I remember on Sunday the 29th of September going in the evening to the New Inn beerhouse, Lower Ince. It was about five minutes to six when I went. I went with Elijah Winstanley and William Kearsley. We all stayed there about an hour and ten minutes and a man named Richard Pritchard was with us. When we left at a quarter past seven I did not hear anything said with regard to Pritchard.

We went across the field to go to the Fox Tavern in Chapel Lane. The railway comes between the New Inn and the Fox Tavern. As we were going along nothing was said about what we were going to do. We all got over the fence onto the railway. We went to some wagons which were in a bit of a siding. I cannot tell where the landing stage is, but there was a wall where we were and the wagons I refer to were standing near the wall. I was on the wall side of the wagons and Kearsley and Winstanley on the other. Kearsley said to me, 'Stop on that side and watch.'

I had been watching about ten minutes when Osborne came on to me. I did not call out to the others. Osborne said to me, 'I have got you now, you devil.' He did not say anything before that. After Osborne came on to me a man rushed past me [Sergeant Kidd?] in the direction of Winstanley and Kearsley who at that time were still on the other side of the wagons from me. After the man rushed round I heard a bit of a struggle coming from the other side of the wagons. I then had a struggle with Osborne, but while I was struggling nobody came up. After I had left Winstanley and Kearsley on the other side of the truck I never saw them again on the railway.

Eventually I got away from Osborne myself. I went away over the canal bridge. I never saw the other two again. I did not hear of them at all on the railway. When I had gone about twenty yards I heard a bit of a scuffle as I was running away home, but I did not know what it was. I ran away home, taking Osborne's staff, but I cannot tell what I did with it.

I remember going to the Fox Tavern between half past nine and ten o'clock the same evening. I there saw

Winstanley and Kearsley. They were in when I got there. I
believe they had the same clothes on as when I last saw
them, except that Winstanley had his hat on. When I went
onto the railway with Winstanley he was wearing a cap.

Halliwell was then shown a cap which he identified as
Winstanley's.

There were minor inconsistencies between Halliwell's
account and that of Detective Osborne, but most of them could
be put down to the well-known fact that no two witnesses ever
recall an event in exactly the same way. If true in substance, the
story Halliwell told was a damning piece of evidence against his
accomplices, but it was just as damning against himself.

The story aroused a deal of interest in court, and there had
already been another sensational event at the same hearing. It
happened as Mr Kershaw, barrister for the prosecution, was
outlining the case before calling witnesses. He began by
announcing that he would offer no evidence against Halliwell
on the charge of murdering Sergeant Kidd but would call him as
a witness to the murder. He would, however, ask the court to
commit Halliwell for trial along with the other two on the charge
of wounding Osborne with intent to do grievous bodily harm
and on certain lesser charges of receiving stolen property.
Following discussion in court, Halliwell was removed from the
dock while the hearing continued against Winstanley and
Kearsley on the major charge.

Continuing his address, Kershaw outlined the events and had
reached the point where Osborne saw a man – identified as
Elijah Winstanley – coming at him with something shiny in his
hand, when Winstanley showed signs of fainting in the dock. A
doctor attended him and he was found a seat in the dock. He
then made a number of loud exclamations, reported as: 'Kill me!
Kill me! Oh, it's murder! I did it! I did it! It's me! I didn't intend
killing him. I did it! It's not our Bill!'

'Our Bill' was a reference to William Kearsley (sometimes
known also as Winstanley) who was Winstanley's half-brother.

After Winstanley had quietened, Mr Kershaw completed his
outline of the evidence and went on to call witnesses.

Plans of the scene of the murder, marked at the points to
which witnesses would refer, were presented by Arthur

Turnbull, Assistant Engineer to the London & North-Western Railway Company. These were accepted in evidence without challenge.

Detective Constable Osborne then gave his account of the events. He was asked certain questions by both prisoners.

Kearsley:	'Did I punch thee?'
Osborne:	'You kicked me.'
Kearsley:	'You're mistaken.'
Winstanley:	'Aye, he is mistaken.'

And at a slightly later stage:

Winstanley:	'Did you say you hit me on the hand?'
Osborne:	'I said I hit a man like you.'

Little analysis is needed to realize how ill-advised these interjections were. The clue is in Osborne's reply, 'I said I hit *a man like you.*' Before then, by using the personal pronouns 'I' and 'me', both prisoners had virtually admitted being the men in question. It hardly mattered to Winstanley, in view of his earlier outburst, but till then Kearsley had done nothing but deny his part. Certainly no solicitor worthy of the name would ever have asked such questions on behalf of clients who were pleading 'Not guilty'.

But this was the lower court hearing, and neither Winstanley nor Kearsley was represented by solicitors as they would have been today. None but the most dedicated opponents of Legal Aid would deny that they should have been represented.

Detective Osborne was then shown two caps and a pair of handcuffs, these items having been found at the scene. He said the caps both belonged to him – one he had been wearing, the other he had loaned to Sergeant Kidd. The latter was seen to be bloodstained. The handcuffs were not his but Sergeant Kidd's.

William Halliwell then gave his evidence, which has already been outlined. He was followed into the witness box by Richard Pritchard, who, it will be recalled, had originally been arrested and charged but against whom no evidence had been offered.

Pritchard corroborated Halliwell's account of the meeting in the New Inn. He said he had left the inn with the other three but had then separated. He saw the others heading towards the railway and heard one of them say he was 'going to get a bag of coal'. Later that evening Pritchard saw Kearsley at the door of his home in Kay's Houses, when he was wearing clothing different from that he had worn at the New Inn.

Police Constable Wilkinson spoke of the finding of four caps at the scene, two by himself and two by other officers. Those of Kidd and Osborne had been identified already; the others were now identified as belonging to Winstanley and Halliwell.

Dr Graham described the injuries to Sergeant Kidd and added the result of his findings at the post-mortem examination.

Dr Roocroft said he had examined the four caps found at the scene. Winstanley's and Kidd's were stained with blood. He had also examined a pair of clogs found at the home of Winstanley and found stains of blood on them. Winstanley himself, this witness added, had a large bruise on his right thumb at the first joint.

When the evidence was completed, Winstanley and Kearsley were committed for trial at the next assizes and taken from the dock. William Halliwell then made a brief appearance and was likewise committed for trial on the lesser charge.

On 17 October the adjourned inquest resumed and was carried to its conclusion. Halliwell was present as both witness and accused. The other two, the coroner said, had been given the opportunity to attend but had declined.

The evidence given contained two new and very important additions. The first was from Dr Graham, again describing the injuries to the dead man. He gave as his opinion that the three most serious stab wounds had been inflicted when Kidd was '... either unconscious or under the control of some person other than the one who stabbed him, and was thus unable to defend himself'.

Halliwell followed the doctor into the witness box. He gave his evidence much as before, but with the following important addition: 'When I saw them afterwards at the Fox Tavern, Winstanley said, "I don't think the man I was agate [struggling] with could live, because I stabbed him many a time, while our Bill holded him." '

'*While our Bill holded him*'! How nicely those few words dovetailed with what Dr Graham had said moments before, and what a spectacle the combined pieces of new evidence must have conjured up in the minds of the coroner and the jury.

It is not recorded whether the court saw anything untoward in the new evidence but, speaking as an onlooker (more than ninety years on), I detect a strong whiff of collusion. The doctor was entitled to express an opinion but, to make use of more modern colloquialisms, I get the feeling that Halliwell was 'putting the verbals' on Winstanley and thereby 'mixing a bottle' for Kearsley.

Those few words were to prove vital at the subsequent trial, and of course they were not objected to at the inquest, since neither Winstanley nor Kearsley was present to object.

The coroner's jury retired, and when they came back into court their foreman announced the verdict: 'That Detective Sergeant Kidd met his death in the discharge of his duties in the goods yard of the London & North-Western Railway Company at Wigan, on 29th September, at the hands of Elijah Winstanley and William Kearsley.'

On being directed by the coroner to state whether they brought a charge of murder or manslaughter, the foreman added: 'Of wilful murder.'

At Liverpool Winter Assizes on Friday 15 November 1895 occurred a rather quaint judicial procedure which has since been discontinued, namely, the charging of the Grand Jury. The Grand Jury's task was to examine the evidence in serious criminal cases and determine if it disclosed a prima-facie case. Once they so found, the case would be remitted to a later date, to be more fully enquired into by a petty jury.

The charges against Winstanley, Kearsley and Halliwell were declared to be well founded, and on Tuesday 26 November 1895 the trial proper began at the same assizes.

Judge Henn Collins presided. Mr Pickford QC and Mr Kershaw appeared for the Crown, Mr McKeand and Mr Cottingham for Winstanley and Kearsley. W. Ambrose Jones watched the case on behalf of William Halliwell.

All three prisoners entered 'Not guilty' pleas to the sundry charges, then Halliwell was removed from the dock, no longer being included in the major charge.

During his outline of the case Pickford stated that up to the time of the lower court hearing the murder weapon had not been traced. However, he would call evidence that on 3 November a group of men had been playing cards in a field adjacent to the railway line, and one of them had found a white-handled, double-bladed penknife. The knife (which he displayed) was bloodstained and *resembled* one Winstanley had – it would not be fair to put it higher than that.

The question for the jury, he went on, was whether the men were guilty of Kidd's death. To him the evidence seemed too terribly clear for any doubt as to Winstanley, but they had no admission from Kearsley that he had anything to do with it. He was, however, engaged in common with Winstanley in the commission of a felony, stealing from railway wagons, and according to the evidence he was also engaged with Winstanley in the struggle. His Lordship would tell them that under those circumstances, if while so doing someone met his death, both men were liable. Supposing the deceased were *held by Kearsley* while he was stabbed by Winstanley, it became a case against Kearsley also.

The evidence was once more presented but need not be retailed here, except for one or two minor matters.

Joseph Glover, an iron-roller, of Canal Bank, Lower Ince, gave evidence of the finding of the knife. David Rogers, a collier, was called to state that he had seen Winstanley in possession of a similar knife. Dr Roocroft said he had examined the knife microscopically and chemically and confirmed that the stains on it were blood. He went on to say that the wounds in Kidd's neck were such as he thought might be caused by the large blade of the knife.

The words Halliwell had attributed to Winstanley came up again when he gave his evidence. At one stage there was a delay when he collapsed in the witness box, and some time passed before he could continue. Cross-examined quite strenuously by McKeand, he stuck to the story entirely.

McKeand's only real triumph came when he asked Halliwell: 'Were you promised anything for coming here as a witness?'

Halliwell replied, 'Mr Macintosh said if I would go in the box and give evidence I would be set free.'

After the prosecution case, Cottingham contended that there was no evidence against Kearsley. His Lordship, however, said he thought there was. Cottingham then announced he would call no defence witnesses.

During his closing speech, Pickford said he would ask the jury first to consider whether – leaving out Halliwell's evidence – there was a sufficiently strong case against the accused. He then outlined the main points of such evidence as came from other sources. The reason he had first treated the case without Halliwell's testimony was, he said, because Halliwell was an accomplice, and evidence of an accomplice called for corroboration. However, he felt Halliwell's story had been corroborated at every step. All the circumstances pointed to the fact that Halliwell had told the truth. He would ask the jury to remember that the statement Halliwell said Winstanley had made ('... our Bill holded him') was *not* evidence against Kearsley, as he could not prove that Kearsley heard it.

'He was only three yards away,' His Lordship interposed.

But Mr Pickford said he still could not prove he had heard, so he asked the jury to dismiss it entirely from their minds – unless, in their opinion, Kearsley heard it and allowed it to pass without contradiction. Then it would be a matter of greatest importance.

McKeand rose to address the jury on behalf of Winstanley. He knew of no duty, he said among other things, more important than the one which by operation of law His Lordship, the bar and the jury had to discharge that day. The jury had the most solemn duty of all. They had to say upon the evidence brought before them whether this man Winstanley should live or die, and he felt perfectly certain that they, as independent and honest gentlemen, while they would not shrink from doing their duty if they thought the man was guilty, would at least do him the honour of listening to the points which he should have to urge on behalf of the unfortunate man, and extend to them their kind and just consideration. If they could consistently with the ends of justice do so, he begged them to spare the life of this man Winstanley.

He also thanked his friends Pickford and Kershaw for the fair way in which they had presented the case to the jury. They had not in the slightest degree prejudiced this man; they had not put forward any evidence that was not right or legal, and Pickford in his opening observations had presented the case in such a way as to give the jury all the assistance he could in arriving at a true, honest and just verdict.

McKeand went on to deal minutely with the evidence against

Winstanley and concluded by appealing to the jury, in the name of all that was honest, right and just, to hesitate before they took away a life which they could not possibly restore.

On behalf of Kearsley, Cottingham urged that there was no evidence outside that of the accomplice Halliwell to connect his client with the murder and, although there might be a certain amount of suspicion, he urged that the jury ought not to rely simply on the evidence of a man who was himself under a charge connected with that case and who had 'stepped into the bus' simply to save himself.

Judge Henn Collins then summed up, telling the jury they must try to find out what share, if any, each of the accused had had in bringing about Kidd's death. One thing was certain: Kidd met his death that night from the result of nine separate wounds inflicted by a sharp instrument. Was there any reason to doubt that both these men were there? Of course, if they accepted the evidence of Halliwell, there was no more to be said about it.

He carefully outlined the rules of evidence as they applied to accomplice testimony and advised the jury that they must view Halliwell's evidence with the greatest possible caution. If they believed the witness, there was no question that the three were there. They had the evidence of Detective Osborne as regards seeing Kearsley, and then there was the bruise on Winstanley's wrist in the place Osborne said he had struck. If there was no reasonable doubt of the three men's being there, the jury would have to consider the question of the share they had in causing the death.

He must tell them in point of law that, if persons were found committing a felony, any member of the public had a right to arrest them. Kidd had that right, whether a constable or not. They would have no right to resist – and Kidd would have the right to use as much force as was reasonably necessary to effect the arrest. If the persons being arrested used such violence as to cause the death of the person arresting, then it was murder.

He dealt again with the matter of Winstanley's alleged remark, '… our Bill holded him'. If Kearsley did not hear it, they must dismiss it from their minds. The doctor's evidence pointed to the wounds' having been inflicted while Kidd was under restraint, but that was a matter of opinion on the doctor's part. If the two men were engaged together in resisting the arrest, and if

Kearsley was holding Kidd while the other man stabbed him, there was very little doubt that the man who held the constable was as much responsible as the man who held the blade.

After deliberating for a quarter of an hour, and without retiring, the jury through its foreman announced their verdict. They found both accused guilty of wilful murder.

Asked if they had anything to say before sentence was passed, Kearsley said, 'I didn't do it.' Winstanley was more voluble. 'It wasn't him,' he said in emphatic tones. 'It was me as did it. Our Bill never touched him; he ran away. Halliwell tells lies. I did it, and that's God's truth.'

Both men were sentenced to death.

Afterwards, Pickford told the court that the other charges against Winstanley and Kearsley, *and all the charges against Halliwell*, would be withdrawn.

His Lordship concurred.

For a moment now, let us consider the effect Winstanley's final assertion must have had on the members of the jury. They had been urged time and again during the course of the trial to accept that the evidence against Kearsley was slender. Now they had heard Winstanley state quite emphatically that, whilst he freely admitted his guilt, Kearsley was innocent – of the murder, at least. They were certainly affected by it. Two members of the jury saw fit to write to solicitors acting for Kearsley, saying in effect that they had been in two minds about Kearsley's guilt. Although they had fallen in with the 'Guilty' verdict, they would not have done so if they had heard Winstanley's assertion beforehand.

Reported in the *Wigan Observer* of 5 October 1895 is an incident which, if true, is quite remarkable. It is said that at 6 p.m. on the night of the murder when Halliwell, Elijah Winstanley, Kearsley and Pritchard visited the New Inn, Lower Ince, they were introduced to James Billington of Farnworth, near Bolton. Billington was well known at that time as the public hangman, and he was there as a guest of the licensee, Mr Openshaw. According to the report, the men shook hands with Billington, and Kearsley remarked that he would not like the hangman to practise his trade on him.

In the outcome, Kearsley did not have to face Billington in his official capacity – but Winstanley did. Petitions were organized on behalf of both men, praying in the case of Kearsley for a free pardon and for Winstanley a commutation of the death penalty. Kearsley's petition succeeded to the extent that his sentence was reduced to penal servitude for life. Winstanley's plea was turned down.

As part of the petition for Winstanley, J.L. Hargreaves, solicitor's clerk, reported as follows:

I had an interview with Elijah Winstanley at Walton Gaol at which no-one was present but Winstanley and myself. I asked Winstanley to tell me the truth – and the whole truth – as to how Detective Kidd met his death.

Winstanley told me that on the night in question he went with Kearsley and Halliwell to the railway trucks for the purpose of taking anything which would be of use to them. He (Winstanley) had a small penknife in his hand and just as he had cut the cord of a package of sweets he was surprised by Detective Kidd who sprang towards him and seized him roughly and threw him to the ground. A struggle took place, he (Winstanley) being underneath. The detective still maintained his hold of the prisoner and Winstanley told the detective he would go quietly if the detective would let him get up. Kidd replied that he would give him something to go for and tried several times to strike the prisoner on the head with a pair of heavy handcuffs, but these blows the prisoner warded off with his hands and arms. It was then, in a moment of frenzy and desperation, that he struck the detective with a knife he held in his right hand, not knowing where the blows fell. Kidd released his hold on prisoner and then lay still. He (Winstanley) then got up and ran away in the belief that the detective was stunned or had fainted.

Winstanley declared that his half-brother, William Kearsley, had previously run away when the detective was first seen and that Kearsley was not present, nor did he take any part in the struggle with the detective. Winstanley further stated that after he had washed his hands he went to Kearsley's house and told him that he had struck the man who had been 'agate' of him with a knife. Upon hearing which, Kearsley was much upset and angry and bitterly complained of his conduct. Winstanley asserted that it was the first time he had ever been on the railway siding for the purpose of theft and he did not know who the detective was in plain clothes, and while admitting the improper use of his penknife he protested most earnestly and emphatically that he did not strike until he himself had been roughly used by the detective, who severely assaulted him and refused to let him rise from the ground.

So it seems Kidd was the aggressor. Except that criminals do tell lies sometimes, even when under sentence of death. And, of course, Kidd could not be there to refute Winstanley's story.

At 8 a.m. on Tuesday 17 December 1895 Winstanley was duly executed at Walton Gaol before the usual large crowd. James Billington officiated. It was said that his conduct in prison had been good, and although he cried whilst being pinioned, he offered no resistance.

William Kearsley served a total of seven years and three months penal servitude. On Saturday 7 February 1903 he was released from Dartmoor Prison and returned to his family.

7 Mute of Malice,
Broughton 1981

Silence in court.

Silence at a time when some audible response would normally have been unfailing.

It was Wednesday 18 November 1981. Mr Justice Lawson was presiding over a session of the Crown Court at Leeds, and in the dock, sitting on the floor with his back to the judge, was thirty-one-year-old labourer John Smith of Burnley. He had refused to acknowledge an indictment charging him with murder and with two counts of kidnapping. Indeed, when the clerk of the court, Jack Hutton, had asked him his name, he had refused to answer.

As would be made clear in later stages of the trial, John Smith was inclined to be talkative. He had something to say on every topic, and when his tongue began to wag, it could be difficult to shut him up. But he was not talking now.

The jury waited. Unknown to them, Mr Ivan Lawrence QC acting for Smith, had already told the court, 'He does not wish to enter a plea because he does not recognize the charge of murder. Nor does he recognize the court.' And when the jury had taken their seats, Judge Lawson said, 'Smith, if you want to know what's going on you had better sit up in a position where you can hear.'

Smith mumbled incoherently but gave no answer, and he remained sitting on the floor of the dock with back turned.

Thus, when the jury retired, having listened to some legal argument but not a word of the evidence in the case, they took with them a question. Was Smith deliberately refusing to answer or had he been struck dumb by some divine visitation? Using the more colourful terms of the law, was he 'mute of malice' or 'mute by visitation of God'?

Imagine the thoughts of Mr Justice Lawson as this pantomime was enacted before him. His jurisdiction did not commonly extend to crimes committed in Lancashire. This case might well have been on the calendar of Preston Crown Court to which Smith had been committed in the first place – and the presiding judge might have been Senior Circuit Judge William Harrison Openshaw. But Judge Openshaw was dead, and Smith was charged with having stabbed him to death.

It was the first time for centuries that a judge had been murdered in office.

The jury returned in two minutes and announced their verdict that Smith was 'mute of malice'. Judge Lawson ordered a plea of 'Not guilty' to be entered on Smith's behalf. He told the jury that, since they had returned a verdict, they would be discharged and the trial would begin before a fresh jury on the following day.

John Smith was a petty thief and burglar with a long-standing grudge against authority, in particular the police and the judiciary. Born in Burnley on 22 October 1949, unmarried and often unemployed, his only permanent address was that of his sister, Brenda Morrison, at 24 Verona Avenue, Burnley. But he was fond of wandering the country and sleeping rough, and when asked his address would usually say, 'NFA' ('no fixed abode'). He lived on state benefits and whatever he could make from 'messing about' with scrap metal. He liked to spend his spare time reading in the public library and was knowledgeable on many subjects.

Before the age of seventeen he was in trouble with the law. At Burnley and Colne County Juvenile Court on Tuesday 26 July 1966, for receiving stolen property, he was fined £10, and for offences of larceny and illegal use of motor vehicles during the following year he was also fined. But there was to be no monetary penalty when, on Thursday 29 February 1968, he appeared at the Lancashire County Intermediate Sessions at Preston and was convicted of housebreaking and larceny, warehouse-breaking and larceny, taking motor vehicles without consent and several minor traffic offences. Nineteen other offences were mentioned and taken into consideration and he was sentenced to a period of Borstal training.

The judge who sentenced him was William Harrison Openshaw.

Thirteen years later, when being interviewed about the judge's murder, Smith was to say to Detective Chief Inspector Jeffrey Meadows, among many similar remarks: 'That bastard gave me eighteen months in Borstal and I couldn't stand it.'

The word 'premeditation' is often used to describe the planning of a murder – and nowhere is it better illustrated than in the words and deeds of John Smith. As avowed by several of his relatives and associates, 'He was always sounding off about Openshaw and Kershaw.' (Judge Philip Kershaw had sentenced him to imprisonment on another occasion.)

'It's people like that Openshaw we should see off,' he told neighbour Francis Burns. 'I think it's about time the I.R.A. started bumping them off.' And again: 'You don't know me, Frank. I'm a bad bastard at times. I'm going to do something big.'

So common were these outbursts, it seems, that people tended to ignore them. 'It was between him and Kershaw,' Smith asserted during that interview thirteen years later. 'Kershaw was going to be the next.' And indeed, there was evidence that he had already made enquiries and obtained Judge Kershaw's address at Lytham.

Smith was a great name-dropper. He railed against 'Mounsey' (Joe Mounsey, Assistant Chief Constable of Lancashire), who, he said, had 'conned' him at Blackpool; against 'top policemen like McNee and Anderton' and against various politicians, including Government ministers. On Thursday 28 May 1981, at Preston Magistrates' Court, in a shock admission supporting Smith's request that reporting restrictions should be lifted, his solicitor, Mr Barrington Black, of Leeds, disclosed that Lord Hailsham had once been a target. Smith had travelled to London in search of Lord Hailsham but at last 'restrained himself'. 'He is a powder keg waiting to erupt,' Barrington Black added.

In Smith's own words. 'Politicians make law, and judges enforce it. They are all pillocks. I wrote to Kilroy Silk and Meacher, [Members of Parliament]. I told them I was going to do someone in and that they could take it any way they liked. They are just like the rest. They capitalize on people like me.'

Most of all, he craved publicity. Speaking of his impending

trial, he said, 'I want the world's press at court. Well, the Nationals, anyway. I want to get over my point of view.'

He had tried to do that seven years earlier when he climbed a 300-foot-high chimney at Burnley General Hospital and for a time defied attempts to bring him down. And then, in August 1980, he went to Blackpool and climbed to the very top of the famous tower, where he stayed for forty-one hours.

'There were underhand dealings on that job,' he was to say later. 'My statement wasn't used.' And when asked, 'What statement?', he explained: 'What I wanted to tell everyone about politicians and the system and police brutality ...' 'The kids wrote "Jump" on the sand,' he said in relation to the Blackpool Tower incident, 'but I'm not that fucking daft. Nobody would have gained but the National Council for Civil Liberties and people like that.'

To his chagrin, Smith was dealt with only for a breach of the peace in the Tower incident, and on Monday 18 August 1980 the Blackpool magistrates bound him over in the sum of £50 to be of good behaviour for two years.

He did not behave well. He was soon in fresh trouble for stealing metal, and a few months later, whilst on bail for the metal theft, he was to breach the binding-over order again, in a spectacular and tragic way.

Judge William Openshaw was sixty-eight years of age, married, with three adult children, one of whom was in practice as a barrister. Born at Hothersall Hall near Ribchester, a lovely old residence and farm on the banks of the River Ribble, he had spent a lifetime practising the law. Educated at Harrow and St Catherine's College, Cambridge, he was called to the bar in 1936. He became a circuit judge in 1958, was Recorder of Preston until 1971 and latterly was a widely known and respected Chairman of the Lancashire County Quarter Sessions, a post formerly held by his father, Sir James Openshaw. He also served as a Deputy Lieutenant of Lancashire. In court circles he was affectionately known as 'Father', a soubriquet he approved of; and though a stern judge, he was compassionate, never ruthless.

Up to the time of his death Judge Openshaw had lived for many years at Park House, 472 Garstang Road, Broughton, near Preston, a large detached house standing in three acres of ground. Among the villagers of Broughton he was extremely popular, and though he loved to spend his time gardening, he would often be seen walking in the village, in deerstalker hat and wellington boots, exercising his dog or waiting to meet his daughter from the school bus. He would appear in the local store, carrying a shopping basket. Locals described him as a gentleman and 'statesman' of the village.

A staunch supporter of Preston North End Football Club, he attended almost every home match and invariably took with him seventy-three-year-old Bob Myerscough, who had formerly worked as his gardener. He treated Myerscough 'like a friend'. 'After the match,' Myerscough remembered, 'we would chat about the game: who had played well and who should be dropped.'

The judge was a courageous man. During the last war, with the rank of major, he led a desperate bayonet charge at Tobruk. He also served for a period in Burma with the Chindits.

Nor was he one to seek anonymity. His name was on the electoral list; his number and address were in the telephone directory. And he scorned security: he had no desire to be guarded. The location of his house was in any case common knowledge.

John Smith knew the house well. As he later admitted, he had secretly visited it several times. 'When I was done for drunk down Woodplumpton Road six months ago,' he said, 'that was after I had been to the house.'

He went there again on the evening of Monday 11 May 1981 and '... hung around, looking for a good vantage-point'. He was carrying a heavy sheath-knife with a bone handle and silver head. He remained there all night, at one stage trying to sleep in a wooden shed beside the house, and for bedding he used a jumper which he had taken from Mrs Openshaw's car.

The next morning, at 8.20 a.m. on a bright spring day, Judge Openshaw left his wife, Emily, herself a magistrate, and walked round to the garage adjoining his house, intending to drive in his green Ford Escort to his duties at Preston Crown Court. Designed to house two cars nose to tail, the garage had an up-and-over door at each end, though the far door was always closed. The pointed roof was supported by crossbeams, and standing on the beams, '... so that he wouldn't see my feet', was John Smith. He had found his vantage-point.

Smith waited until the judge had walked right into the garage. 'I didn't want to do him from behind,' he told Chief Inspector Meadows later, 'because I wanted to see his face when I stabbed him – and I wanted him to see me.' Choosing his time, he leaped down and faced the judge, and as he described it later in a long voluntary statement: 'He looked at me startled and didn't know what to say. I said, "Now then, I've got you." He said, "Oh no. Please." I then lunged at him ...'

The attack was swift and vicious. The judge tried to defend himself, and some of his injuries were 'defence' wounds, but Smith stabbed him at least twelve times in the thigh, side, chest and face. Four times the knife penetrated the judge's skull, once to a depth of five inches. In his evidence at the trial, Dr John Gordon Benstead, Home Office Pathologist, described these as 'blows delivered with great force'.

Leaving his victim close to death, Smith then climbed into the judge's Ford Escort and tried to start the engine with the keys which had been left in the ignition, his clear intention being to drive away. But the engine did not fire, and at that moment Mrs Openshaw came out of the house. She had heard the sound of an engine, which was expected, but there had been other sounds, one of which might have been a faint 'Help!' Coming to the garage, she saw her husband's car – and a stranger at the wheel, revving the engine. She was unaware of her husband's plight and sensibly ran back to the house to telephone the police.

'I was glad she ran into the house,' Smith told Meadows later. 'I didn't want to have to kill her.'

But Mrs Openshaw's intervention obliged him to abandon his attempt to steal the car. He ran away across a paddock and through the garden of a nearby house into Whittingham Lane.

Two doors away, schoolboy Gary Anthony Hilton was in the kitchen of his home, 2 Whittingham Lane, Broughton. The dog had been let out and, hearing it begin to bark, he looked out of the window in time to see a man step over the hedge from Judge Openshaw's garden into the back garden of 4 Whittingham Lane. The man, whom Gary took to be a builder, walked down the side of the house towards the lane and passed from sight.

Alerted by Mrs Openshaw's call, the police went to Park House. Police Sergeant David Malcolm Hartley was first on the scene, and going into the garage he saw the Ford Escort parked there, facing the far door, with its ignition switched on and the heater on blow. In front of the car he saw the judge lying on his stomach, his head covered with blood. The door, normally kept closed, had been opened slightly, and its lower edge was resting on the judge's neck. The sergeant pulled the top of the door, opening it wide, and began to apply first aid, whilst other officers were sending for an ambulance. Inspector Peter Greenhough, who had arrived within seconds, noticed that apart from the head wounds the judge was bleeding badly from the side, and he and other officers cut away part of the judge's upper clothing to locate the wound and attempt to stem the bleeding. At that time Judge Openshaw was still alive, but he stopped breathing shortly afterwards.

The police surgeon, Dr Martin Joseph Roche Ryan, was called to the scene and after examining the judge confirmed that he was dead. The body was removed to the mortuary at Sharoe Green Hospital, Preston. A major police operation was soon under way, led by Detective Superintendent Ray Rimmer, but by then Smith had made his escape in dramatic circumstances.

A company director, Walter James Barry Hide, of Knowle Cottage, Camforth Hall Lane, Goosnargh, had left home about 8.15 a.m. that day. He was driving his car, a metallic green Austin Maxi Highline, registered number GFR 564 S, along Whittingham Lane towards the Broughton traffic lights at the junction with Garstang Road. When he came close to the junction, he saw a man – undoubtedly Smith – burst out of the driveway of a house on his left and run into the road, waving frantically. Assuming there was some emergency, Walter Hide slowed almost to a standstill, whereupon Smith opened the nearside passenger door and jumped in. As he did so, he pulled from the left-hand side of his waistband a sheath-type knife. Holding the knife in his left hand on his lap, pointing at Hide, he said: 'Just do as I say and you won't get hurt.'

What followed was an unexpected and nightmare ride for Hide, which was to end 130 miles away, in Scotland.

'Turn right and get on the motorway,' he was told, and although he explained that the motorway could be reached more quickly by turning left, Smith ignored the advice. So they turned right and headed north along the A6, Garstang Road. Smith seemed very agitated, but talkative. 'I don't suppose you've ever been hi-jacked before,' he said. 'It's not a pleasant experience.' Shortly after that he said, 'The guy had it coming to him. About thirteen years ago he sent me down to Borstal.'

When they came to the turning for the Trough of Bowland, he ordered Hide to take that road, but they were going fast and the order came too late. They turned onto the M6 at Forton and continued northwards. When they were approaching the service area at Burton, Hide explained that the car was low on petrol, and Smith agreed that they should fill up at the services. At that stage he picked up Hide's blue turtle-neck sweater which was lying on the seat, spat on his hands and rubbed them with the sweater. He then covered the knife with the sweater, still keeping it pointed at Hide. 'You fill it up,' he said. 'But no tricks.'

There was no opportunity for Hide to try any tricks. Smith stayed close against him at the petrol pump and then told him to go to the kiosk and buy some cigarettes. 'Number Six,' Smith said to the girl in the kiosk. 'King size. And a box of matches.' Hide paid for the petrol and the cigarettes with notes from his wallet, and later Smith took from him the rest of the money.

Back on the motorway, Smith directed Hide to make for Carlisle. 'It will be out now,' he said, 'and if there are any road blocks, put your foot down and drive through.' On Smith's instructions Hide drove at a steady 70 mph. They discussed routes and the advantages of using side roads, but Hide persuaded him against side roads, feeling safer among traffic.

'Take that road,' Smith ordered when they were approaching the turn-off for the A69, so Hide left the M6 and headed towards Newcastle-on-Tyne. By now Smith had relaxed. He was smoking and had put the knife down on his lap. 'He had it coming to him,' he said once more. 'You'll probably know him. Openshaw.'

One of the subjects they discussed during the long journey was the thorny one of how Smith should get rid of Hide. One plan was that he should tie Hide up and put him in the boot. But on an Austin Maxi there is no boot. 'Why not just drop me somewhere and I'll give you half an hour to escape?' Hide suggested, but Smith would have none of that. Meantime they reached Newcastle and toured the city in a desultory way before Smith decided they must head for Berwick-on-Tweed. There was another stop for petrol, and again Hide was watched too closely to have any chance of escaping or giving a warning. They followed the A68 Edinburgh road, bypassing Jedburgh, and some twenty miles short of Edinburgh Smith chose to turn off onto a side road.

The problem of his parting company with Hide had still not been resolved, but now the suggestion came from Smith that he should tie Hide to a tree: Hide, no doubt seeing his own salvation in it, supported the scheme. So a suitable spot was found and Smith used the cable from jump leads in the car to tie Hide's wrists behind him with his arms round the trunk of a tree. This was apparently done in amicable fashion, with a deal of discussion about whether Hide should be left sitting or standing. Hide elected to sit, and Smith agreed. At one stage, Smith actually handed the knife to Hide and told him to cut the jump lead cable with it.

While this was happening, Smith asked Hide his name. He replied, 'Jim.' Smith said, 'It's a bad thing to kill someone', an ambiguous remark that might have referred to the earlier event or, dreadfully, might have revealed an intent to kill Hide. But the moment passed, and once Hide was secured, Smith drove off in the Maxi – but not before promising that he would phone someone in an hour's time and have Hide released.

However, Hide struggled and released himself in shorter time. He walked to the nearest house, that of Helen Jack, 15 Crookston Mains Cottages, Heriot, on the B6368 Gilston road, and telephoned the police from there.

Detective Constable John Henry Clarke, Lothian & Borders Police, went to Crookston Mains and spoke to Hide, who showed him the tree to which he had been tied. He also produced pieces of cut cable and showed the officer marks on his wrists made by the cable. Clarke took full details and circulated a message with a description of Smith and the missing car.

About 1.50 p.m. on the same day, Tuesday 12 May 1980, Police Constables James Haines Wilson and Gordon Smith, also Lothian & Borders, were patrolling in a police car in Melrose Burgh when they were instructed by radio to keep a look-out for the Austin Maxi and if possible detain the occupant. They drove along the A68 Edinburgh to Newcastle road towards St Boswells and about 2.04 p.m. spotted the car ahead, turning away from them as it emerged from the A6091 onto the A68, heading south towards Jedburgh. They radioed in and were instructed to follow the car to the next checkpoint.

Their speed was quite sedate at first, but then the Maxi driver, evidently realizing they were on his tail, increased speed, and the chase was on. At Cleekimin, Jedburgh, Police Constables Henderson and Nichol had set up a road block, and Henderson stood in the road, signalling the Maxi to stop. The Maxi slowed to about 40 mph, then suddenly accelerated, forcing Henderson to leap out of its path. PC Nichol gave chase in a Rover police car, drew in front of the Maxi and forced it to stop some 500 yards south of the junction with A68 and the A698 Hawick/Kelso road. The driver got out, crossed the road verge, climbed over a fence and began to run across a field.

Constables Wilson and Smith gave chase. Wilson overtook the driver, grabbed him and pinned him to the ground. Smith saw a horn-handled knife in the driver's waistband and seized it. The man was handcuffed, placed in a police car and taken to Jedburgh police station. He identified himself as John Smith, born on 22 October 1949, of no fixed abode.

After being strip-searched, Smith was taken to Lothian & Borders Police Headquarters at Wilton Hill, Hawick. He was locked in a cell, and the Lancashire Police were informed.

Detective Chief Inspector Meadows, Detective Inspector Roy Slater and Detective Constable Michael Arnold travelled to Scotland and interviewed Smith at Hawick. It was a very long question-and-answer interview, during which Smith was far from mute and showed considerable malice. Certain outrageous statements he made have been mentioned earlier. There were others.

But he was cagey at first.

'My mind's a blank,' he told them. 'I don't remember anything. I take tablets, you know.'

'What sort?' he was asked.

'DGs. Tuinol. Valium.'

'If you mean distalgesics,' Meadows said, 'they are only pain-killers. They won't make your mind a blank.'

'But I take a lot,' Smith said.

After more fencing of this sort, Smith began to talk about 'this fellow from Preston, who owns the car'. He admitted having threatened the man with his knife, forcing him to drive to Scotland. But the spell of confession was brief. He turned the subject to police 'conning' and police brutality. 'Look at this,' he said, showing handcuff scratches on his wrist.

And then he went back to 'I can't remember', and there was more verbal fencing, until Meadows said to him, 'You've started to sweat, John. Tell me what these hands have done today.'

'I just wanted to make a protest,' Smith said. 'I've come to realize that peaceful protests don't work. You've got to be prepared to resort to violence. I wrote to Kilroy Silk and Meacher ...'

And so on, until Meadows said to him: 'Why did you do it, John?'

'Because he was the bastard who sent me down the first time – on five charges ... I remember the day. It was leap year. It was 29th February 1968. That was the start of it all. I only had two previous [convictions] and I had only been fined before. That bastard gave me eighteen months in Borstal ... He's sent everyone down. Sometimes twenty a day.'

'Why kill him, John?' Meadows probed. 'He was an old man. You didn't give him a chance.'

Smith was contemptuous.

'What did you want me to do? Give him the fucking knife and then he could stab me? The bastard has stabbed enough people in the back in his time.'

After that, the words began to pour out. He had been thinking about killing Openshaw for thirteen years. He had found the judge's address in the electoral roll at Preston and had visited the house several times during the months preceding the crime. He said Judge Philip Kershaw was 'going to be next' because 'He gave me 2½ years as well.' He knew where Kershaw lived at Lytham because he had looked it up.

At one stage, he said, 'If ever I get out of here, you'd better watch it.'

'You mean me personally?' Meadows wondered.

'No, not you. But those top policemen, McNee and Anderton.'

He went on to discuss the merits of a possible defence of 'diminished responsibility', to compare the British legal system with that of the United States of America and to comment on recent statements by various politicians.

Then he said: 'I'm not ashamed of what I've done. I'm glad I killed him. If I hadn't killed him I would have felt like shooting myself.' After a pause, he added, 'In some respects he's better off than I am.'

Asked if he wished to make a statement, he said: 'I'm not sure about a statement because you won't write down exactly what I say.'

'We're writing down exactly what you say,' he was assured.

'When I said the trial judge was a pillock, I didn't mean it that way. He's just a puppet of the establishment.'

But he was talking more openly about the murder now. He described his route to the judge's house on the eve of the fatal day. Before taking up his 'vantage point' on the roof beams of the garage he had checked the Ford Escort, '... to make sure it was his and not hers'. He had found letters in the car addressed to Judge Openshaw. He had opened the boot to see if his wig was there. Disappointingly, it was not.

Standing on the garage roof beams, he had heard someone come to the house, 'the milk lad, or the paper lad', and he had waited until he heard Openshaw himself coming to the garage. He described in some detail the attack on the judge and the moment when Mrs Openshaw appeared to surprise him. He went on: 'He was lying on the floor. I just ran off. I ran round onto the road and stopped that car. You know the rest.'

Shown the bone-handled sheath-knife, Smith admitted it was his. He said he had bought it some time before, at Cockers' shop in Burnley. He had thrown the sheath out of the window of the Maxi somewhere on the M6 as they had headed north.

This was untrue, however. The sheath was later found beside the Gilston road (B6368) not far from the spot where he had left Walter Hide tied to the tree. Ann Rae, a student, found it, and Thomas George Dun, of Crookston Mains Farm, Hawick, received it and handed it to the police.

In the end he did make a voluntary statement, though he haggled about the formalities.

'I've had statements written for me before, and some things are said which are not quite right and what I don't mean.'

'You can write it yourself,' he was told, and Detective Chief Inspector Meadows went on to explain to him the procedure for recording such a statement.

'I'll write it myself,' he decided.

The result was a document which, apart from the witnessing signatures of the police officers present, was entirely in Smith's own handwriting: the opening caution formula, the body of the statement and the standard endorsement at the foot. In substance it was identical with the story he had told the officers verbally. It included the words: 'In a way, the only winners are the police. Both me and Openshaw are the losers. I don't really know who's the luckier, him or myself, as I'll now be incarcerated for the rest of my life.'

Smith came back on song when the subject of notifying a solicitor to act for him was raised.

'I don't want any fucking cowboys from Burnley who work hand in glove with the police,' he said. 'If I go back to England, I'll have Barrington Black.'

All this in Scotland, and then the somewhat technical rigmarole made necessary by inconsistencies between Scottish and English law: a brief court appearance, the formal release of Smith from custody, the execution of a warrant previously obtained in England and the retaking of the prisoner by English officers.

'I've nothing to say,' he said ludicrously when the warrant was read over to him.

During the long drive back to Preston he had plenty to say.

'It's a pity they've done away with topping.' (Hanging.)

'But I looked it up under the Treason Act, 1351. Openshaw doesn't qualify as a King's Justice. What have I got to look forward to? Spending the rest of my life inside. Still, it was worth it. I had considered all that before I did him.'

And in a later burst: 'If he hadn't sent me down ... I wouldn't have killed him ... and I wouldn't be the monster I am.'

'You think you're a monster, John?' Meadows commented.

'Anybody who can kill anyone in cold blood is a monster. At least, that's what everyone will say.'

Still later, he grumbled about nobody ever treating him fair: 'Even the fellow I hi-jacked broke his promise. He said he wouldn't try to get free. I could have killed him, but I didn't. I trusted him. I even handed him the knife.'

And he discussed his intention of entering a 'guilty' plea: 'I'm not going to cause that Openshaw widow any more distress,' he said.

Strange that a man so loquacious should later choose to be silent when arraigned. No divine power had locked his tongue. There can be little doubt that the first jury at Leeds Crown Court had been absolutely correct in adjudging Smith 'mute of malice', and although the recorded plea was 'Not guilty', that was not anything Smith had ever said but a legal formality, imposed because he chose to say nothing.

On Thursday 19 November 1981 the case was continued at Leeds Crown Court. The indictment charged Smith with three counts: of murdering Judge Openshaw, of stealing and unlawfully carrying away Mr Walter James Barry Hide against his will, and of unlawfully and injuriously imprisoning Mr Hide and detaining him against his will in some secret and private place, all charges brought under Common Law.

Mr Justice Lawson still presided. Michael McGuire and D. Sumner prosecuted on behalf of the Crown. Smith was represented by Ivan Lawrence QC and Louise Godfrey.

Smith's attitude had not changed. Three jurors were challenged by the defence and replaced. Smith continued to sit on the floor of the dock and repeatedly shouted that he wanted to be taken to the cells below. There were other interruptions as the various witnesses were called.

Apart from Smith's confession, there was plenty of evidence to link him with the crime. The sheath-knife matched the wounds in the judge's body. Expert blood-grouping showed that the stains on the knife, on Smith's clothing and on Hide's blue turtle-neck sweater accorded with the blood of the victim and not with Smith's. Dr Ryan, the police surgeon, had examined Smith and reported that he found no injury or abnormality.

Dust marks on the garage beams and floor confirmed Smith's presence there in circumstances such as he had himself outlined. He was identified by witnesses as the man seen running from the house – and of course Hide's evidence and that of the Scottish police officers formed an all but continuous account of the flight from the scene and Smith's movements up to the time of his arrest.

Enquiries had been made into Smith's medical history, and Dr Sharma of the Psychiatric Department at Chorley Hospital confirmed that during August and September 1973 Smith had been an inmate of Whittingham Hospital and under his care, having been committed there under Section 60 of the Mental Health Act, following a conviction for assault. Whilst there, the doctor said, Smith had been rude, aggressive, bloody-minded, quick-tempered and easily brought to rage. He was suspicious of all authority, felt everyone was against him and constantly complained of 'imaginary' illnesses which were no more than attention-seeking ploys. Smith had a behavioural problem, the doctor said, but he was not mentally ill.

His family practitioner, Dr Kenyon, of Burnley Medical Centre, had known him for twenty-five years. He had treated Smith officially for nervous debility but believed him to be a dangerous psychopath and had tried to have him committed. Smith, he said, hated the police and the legal system.

At the close of the evidence, submissions and summing-up, the jury retired to consider its verdicts. When the jury returned to court, the foreman announced verdicts of 'Guilty' on the first two charges. Mr Justice Lawson directed that the jury be discharged from giving a verdict on the third charge.

Smith had not finished yet.

It was announced that he had dismissed his barrister, Ivan Lawrence QC, and wanted a statement, which he had written *before* the crime, to be read to the court on his behalf by Louise Godfrey. Mr Justice Lawson agreed but warned sternly: 'I'm not going to allow this Court to be used for his attention-seeking activities. He is a very dangerous man.'

In the statement, Smith had written: 'No court over here has the right to try me. I won't get a fair hearing when nearly every member associated with the Crown Court system knew Judge Openshaw personally. I want to go to the International Court of Human Rights ...'

'You are going to humiliate and degrade people, aren't you, you sadist,' he told the judge, as two prison officers hauled him to his feet to listen to the passing of sentence.

On the first charge he was sentenced to life imprisonment with a direction that he should serve a minimum of twenty-five years, and on the second to five years imprisonment, to run concurrently.

'I won't forget you,' he shouted to Judge Lawson as he was being taken from the dock. 'I'll cut your throat when I get out.'

And, typically, he had yet another last word.

'I am not sorry for what I have done,' he is reported to have said after the case. 'I would do the same again tomorrow.'

8 Charlie Peace – Or Was It?
Old Trafford 1876

The school building programme of eighty years ago included fine new municipal schools to be built on open land bordering Oswald Street, Chorlton-cum-Hardy, and as the site chosen was rough, undulating country, a great deal of clearing work and excavation was needed to lay the foundations of the buildings. This included the draining and infilling of a number of water-filled clay pits.

Among the many workmen engaged on the project was a man named Fay. On Friday 6 September 1907 he was digging with his spade in the mud of one of the clay pits when – as reported in the *Daily Dispatch* the following day – he made a discovery that was to throw new light on a thirty-one-year-old murder, a murder for which one man was convicted and later pardoned when another man – the notorious Charlie Peace – confessed to it.

The item Fay unearthed – which for years had lain under ten feet of water and several feet of mud – was a pistol. It had a single barrel, octagonal on the outside, and a heavy ebony stock. The metal parts had once been silvered, and traces of the plating were still to be seen. The haft bore a silver monogram shield, but the inscription on it – if there had been one – was entirely worn away. The weapon was of the type fired by percussion cap, and the bore was about three-eighths of an inch in diameter, or as near to .444 calibre as in those days would not matter.

The origins of the pistol were never established with certainty but, after examining and testing it, the police made a strong assumption that it might have been used on Wednesday 2

August 1876 at nearby West Point, Whalley Range, to murder a policeman engaged in the execution of his duty.

Three considerations gave rise to this belief. First, the weapon used to shoot the policeman was known to have been of the percussion-cap type; secondly, the bullet found in his body was of .444 calibre, and thirdly, the records showed that the police had unsuccessfully dragged the clay pits on the Oswald Street site in the belief that the murder weapon might have been thrown into one of them.

The murdered man was Police Constable Nicholas Cock, of the Lancashire Constabulary, stationed at Old Trafford. Cock was born at Liskeard, Cornwall, in 1855 and was in his twenty-first year when he joined the Force on 13 December 1875. Before that he had worked as a miner in various parts of the country, latterly for a mining engineering company at Copley, Cumberland. He soon became known as 'the little Bobby', and not surprisingly, since he was only five feet 7½ inches tall and built proportionately.

Cock, a single man, was posted to Old Trafford on New Year's Day 1876, having held the office of constable for just eighteen days. Presumably he gave satisfaction in his work during the few months that followed, though the only surviving record of his zeal is that in July of that year he arrested a number of men for drunkenness. One of those men was John Habron, an Irishman, and he told Cock that if he was brought to court for the offence he would shoot the constable before midnight.

Habron was indeed summonsed, and it seems that following his conviction and fine at Strangeways Magistrates' Court he faced Cock again and repeated his words.

The constable must have been impressed by the threat. He went at once and reported it to his superintendent, James Bent.

Bent was a man of great renown, then and since. During his successful career, which spanned fifty-three years, he dealt with many serious crimes. But he is best remembered as the organizer and driving force behind a soup kitchen for poor children which he started in 1878. It ran for many years – supplying up to 150,000 meals annually – and continued long after the superintendent's death in 1901. Much has been written about these matters, not the least flattering by Bent himself.

In 1876, when Constable Cock came to Bent with his story of

the threat, the superintendent was inclined to make light of it. 'Take no notice,' he advised. 'They are only blowing off steam.'

But for once Bent was mistaken. Within a few hours Cock was dead, killed by a bullet fired from a pistol, in the following circumstances.

Approaching midnight on 2 August, Cock and Police Constable Beanland were patrolling together on foot in Upper Chorlton Road at West Point when they saw a man come from Whalley Range, cross Seymour Grove and enter the garden of a house. The time and the man's furtive manner led them to the view that he must be a burglar, so the two separated, Beanland to head the man off, Cock to cover his retreat.

The man doubled back, climbed over a wall and – it seems – fell into the arms of Constable Cock.

Seconds later, Beanland heard two shots and, on running towards the sounds, found his colleague fatally wounded.

When he heard about this, Superintendent Bent rushed to the scene, but the injured man was too far gone to identify his assailant or describe the attack on him. He was rushed to the surgery of a local doctor, where he died within half an hour.

Of the two bullets fired, one had lodged in the constable's body and was recovered during the subsequent post-mortem examination. The other had struck the wall close to a local feature known as the Jutting Stone, leaving a tell-tale mark.

Superintendent Bent led the ensuing hunt, and in view of what Cock had told him only that day, it is hardly surprising that he was soon knocking on the door of an outhouse at nearby Firs Farm, where John Habron lived with his brothers, William and Frank. It is doubtful if Bent even bothered to knock; no doubt he burst in. At any rate, with other officers he entered the outhouse and in the light of his lamp saw the three brothers lying in their beds. When he roused them, he faced three naked men. He ordered them to dress 'in the clothes they had worn when they went to bed', and when they had done so, he had them secured with handcuffs.

'Now mind what I am about to say to you,' he said. 'You three are charged with the murder of Constable Cock.'

The only reply he received was from John Habron, and Bent noted the words and was to make use of them later.

'I was in bed at the time,' John said.

It was not uncommon in those days for suspects to be 'arrested', and it does not seem to have mattered to Bent that Constable Beanland had reported seeing only one man. The superintendent cast his net wide – and indeed the case might have ended differently had he arrested only John, the man who had threatened the constable.

Contrary to Bent's arresting words, Frank Habron was never 'charged' with the crime. But John and William Habron were, and after preliminary hearings they appeared for trial in November 1876 at Manchester Assizes, Mr Justice Lindley presiding.

The evidence against them was not particularly strong in any specific area, but the circumstances formed a credible chain. Constable Beanland described the man he and Cock had seen and presumed to be a burglar. The description was sparse, but broad enough to encompass either John or William Habron. A man named Simpson spoke of having been with the two constables a short time before the shooting, though what value that evidence bore is difficult to see. Other police officers gave corroborating evidence of searches at the scene and the arrest of the Habrons, and a local boot-maker was called to describe footwear worn by the brothers, which Bent had recovered from their home.

That apart, the evidence consisted largely of Superintendent Bent's findings and, though they were carefully and honestly presented, it has to be said that some of them would not be admitted under modern rules of evidence.

He began by relating John Habron's threat to Cock, as outlined to him by the constable – a threat which had assumed importance in view of the constable's death so soon afterwards. He said that at the scene of the shooting the footmarks of several people had been found. One of these indicated that the walkers had been heading towards Firs Farm. He covered the marks with boxes, for more detailed examination in daylight.

In dealing with the arrest he made a strong point of John Habron's remark 'I was in bed at the time', uttered when told he would be charged. These words were significant in themselves, he pointed out, since no time had yet been mentioned.

The outhouse in which he found the brothers apparently sleeping had been in darkness when he entered, but just before that, Bent said, he was convinced he had seen a light reflected from the room. 'I examined a candle. It was softer than natural, as though it had recently been burning.'

He had later experimented to show that the candle had been lit immediately before he burst into the outhouse.

'I caused a lighted candle to be placed in the outhouse,' he told the court, 'and on going into the road I could see the reflection on the privy wall which is in front of the window, and when I went to the gate I could see the light in the window.'

The boots of all three men were examined and, 'William's boots were wettest and slutchiest.' (The word 'slutch', meaning mud or mire, seems to be solely a Lancastrian dialect word.)

More importantly, William's left boot had been compared with one of the marks Bent had noticed and protected at the scene of the murder, and it appeared to correspond. 'I counted the nails in the impression and had it measured. The nails in the outside row were very close together, and I could not count them, but the inside row I counted. There were fourteen on one side and thirteen on the other. I counted the nails in his left boot and they corresponded. There is a plate on the heel of the boot, and that plate was shown in the impression.'

Other marks at the scene were less detailed, but, 'As far as I was able to make comparison, they corresponded.'

The boot-maker supported this evidence and confirmed that the nail pattern was 'very peculiar' for a strong boot.

By this time, Bent seemed to be making out a stronger case against William Habron than against John, his original suspect, and this must have impressed the jury since, after deliberating for some time, they acquitted John Habron and convicted William.

On such evidence it is doubtful whether either man would have been convicted today, though in fairness to the jury they had a little more to go on – supplied by the defence.

Against the advice of their counsel, the Habrons had tried to establish an alibi by calling witnesses – and those witnesses, by shrewd questioning, were shown to be lying.

William Habron, just eighteen years old, was sentenced to hang. However, a petition for mercy was signed by many local residents and submitted to the Home Secretary, who commuted the sentence to one of life imprisonment. But for such leniency, this story would have ended there, or at least there would have been little point in the gesture that was to follow.

'*Vox Populi – Vox Dei*. ('The voice of the people is the voice of God.') Those same local residents and many others also, having petitioned for the convicted man, now had their say about the courage and devotion to duty shown by Constable Nicholas Cock. A sum of money was raised by public subscription and used to purchase a memorial headstone which was erected over his grave in the churchyard of St Clement's Church, Chorlton-cum-Hardy.

Two years later, a man using the name John Ward was arrested in London for burglary and for shooting a London policeman with intent to murder. It soon emerged that 'John Ward' was none other than the infamous Charlie Peace, already wanted in Sheffield for the murder of a man named Albert Dyson.

For the London crime he was sentenced at the Central Criminal Court to penal servitude for life – and then he was taken in custody to Leeds, where he was arraigned at the assizes on the charge of murdering Dyson. On that charge he was found guilty and sentenced to death.

Lying in the death cell at Leeds Prison, Peace astounded everyone by confessing to the murder of Constable Nicholas Cock. Peace was already famed as a liar and a glory-seeker, but this confession was evidently more than a piece of conceit. He sent for a clergyman and in his presence wrote a long statement which he signed and the clergyman witnessed.

Now that he must forfeit his own life, the statement said, there was no point in further secrecy, and he thought it right to clear the young man William Habron, who was innocent of the murder. Recalling the incident, Peace said he had intended to break into the house in Chorlton-cum-Hardy but was spotted by two policemen and in trying to escape ran into the arms of one of them. There was a scuffle and he fired twice. The first time he aimed deliberately wide in order to scare the constable, but the second shot was true and found its mark.

He drew a map of the scene to describe his movements and went on to say that, after he heard that the Habrons had been charged with the crime, he was interested. So he decided to attend their trial at the assizes. He was present, sitting in the public gallery, on 28 November 1876, when William Habron was convicted and sentenced to death.

There seems to have been no time in Charlie Peace's adult life when he was not on the run, and if it is true that he sat in the public gallery throughout an assize, that was a remarkable show of audacity. Even more remarkable is another related matter. On 29 November, the very next day, he was a-burgling in Sheffield and shot dead Albert Dyson.

But was Peace's story true?

Clearly he knew many details about the Chorlton-cum-Hardy murder, but if he had been present at the trial, he could easily have learned them there. And whilst it is true he had nothing to gain by keeping his secret, he had nothing to lose either, and to a man such as Peace the idea of overthrowing an official judgment might have seemed a rewarding caprice.

The Chief Constable of Lancashire, C.G. Legge, clearly had his doubts. In a letter to the Under-Secretary of State, Home Office, dated 23 February 1879, he expressed some of them:

> ... I yesterday visited the place where Police Constable Cock was murdered ... and have endeavoured to sift the truth of Peace's statement. With regard to the plan drawn by him, I have to inform you that it is substantially correct, though several inaccuracies exist in it, and is such a plan as a burglar well acquainted with the district – as Peace has been for a long time, having twice been convicted of burglaries committed in the neighbourhood in the years 1859 and 1866 – might easily draw.
>
> As regards his account of what occurred on the night in question, I would observe that it corresponds in great measure *with the evidence given at the trial of the brothers Habron*, but he is incorrect in saying there were two civilians standing with the two constables at the Ducking [this should be Jutting] Stone ... the witness Simpson was the only one there that night, and he had left the constables and gone in the direction of Brook's Bar before the man whom PCs followed did so.
>
> Peace is also wrong as to the gate which the man was seen to enter ... and Constable Beanland also says he does not believe it possible for a man to have made his escape in

the direction indicated by Peace without him seeing him, as it took less time for him to reach the gate from where he was standing when the shots were fired than for a man to have got out of sight as Peace says he did.

This constable is sure that he saw the flashes and heard the report of a pistol as shown on the official plan and not on Peace's plan, and certainly the mark on the Jutting Stone would be more consistent with shots fired as Beanland says than as indicated by Peace. Peace's account of his escape is not a very consistent one, as he omits a road ... altogether in his plan and represents himself as going through a garden and over a wall where stables really stand ...

It is true, however, that men were working day and night at a sewer in the fields and had a fire burning ... It also appears that Peace and William Habron are about the same size, 5' 3½''.

I propose taking the bullet found in Cock's body to Leeds tomorrow, with a view to ascertaining if it could, or is likely to have been fired from Peace's pistol ... If it were admissible to put any questions to Peace I think there are one or two I might ask him with reference to the houses in Seymour Grove, the answers to which might tend to prove the truth or falsehood of his statement.

Legge closed his letter with a broad hint: 'There was much that could not be made evidence that occurred at the time of the murder which seemed to fasten the guilt on one or more of the Habrons, but it seems difficult to perceive what motive Peace can have in charging himself with it unless he was really the perpetrator of it.'

On 5 March 1879 Legge wrote again to pass on some gossip which had reached him through the Chief Constable of Manchester, Captain Palin, which suggested that Peace was in Manchester 'about the time Fish was tried for the murder of the little girl at Blackburn' (28 July 1876).

'There can I think be little doubt,' he wrote, 'that Peace was in the neighbourhood ... as a report of the robbery of a concertina was made to Salford Police on 26/4/1876, which concertina was found among Hannah Peace's property.'

And tossing a crumb on the scale in favour of Peace's confession being true, in discussing information from 'one of the criminal classes,' he closed the letter: '... he says Peace was commonly talked of as the murderer of Cock among those with whom he associated.'

One thing is sure: the Home Secretary was sufficiently persuaded by the evidence he had that there were good grounds for believing William Habron to be innocent. He granted Habron a free pardon and an award of £800.

The comparison of the bullet from Cock's body with a pistol found in Peace's possession gave a positive result within the limits of ballistics as they were practised then. James Woodward, gunmaker, of 64 St James Street, London, averred that the 'Cock' bullet was exactly the same as the 'Robinson' and 'Dyson' bullets (Robinson being the London policeman). The marks of the grooving seemed to compound accurately with test samples fired by him from Peace's pistol. 'They are cast bullets,' he said, 'and considering they are cast, their weights agree very closely.'

So – what of the other pistol, the one found thirty years later at Chorlton-cum-Hardy? Was that Peace's pistol too? And if so, why did he throw it away? He did not throw away the pistol used to kill Dyson in Sheffield but took it with him to London and used it again on Robinson. Why, then, would he throw away a valuable weapon after shooting Cock?

Or was it really Habron's pistol, and had *he* used it to kill Cock? And had he then thrown it into the clay pit?

Then again, perhaps the later pistol belonged to neither Habron nor Peace but to some unknown criminal.

In other words, there is still doubt about who actually killed Cock, and it is unlikely ever to be removed.

The tombstone erected in Constable Cock's memory, having been neglected for some time, was removed from St Clement's, Chorlton-cum-Hardy, in November 1956. It has been completely renovated and now stands in the grounds of Lancashire Constabulary Headquarters.

The inscription reads:

TO THE MEMORY OF NICHOLAS COCK.
An able and energetic officer of the County Constabulary

who on 2nd August, 1876, while engaged in the faithful discharge of his duty, was cruelly assassinated.

This monument was raised by voluntary contributions: the subscribers consisting of magistrates, the officers and men of his own force and citizens in general who felt that some public tribute was due to the name of one who, while in his private capacity deserved well of those who knew him, for zeal and fidelity in his office was worthy of honourable remembrance by all.

Be thou Faithful unto Death and he will
give Thee a Crown of Life.

9   The Story of a Gun, Knowsley 1942-52

As reigning monarch, HM The Queen is Duke of Lancaster, a truth jealously flaunted in the county and always celebrated at dinner as the port is passed and the Loyal Toast proposed. For Lancastrians are Royalists by and large, and if the Queen herself does not live in Lancashire, she is well represented there, for the Stanleys, earls of Derby, have had their principal seat at Knowsley Hall, near Prescot, since the fourteenth century.

Knowsley Hall, only a few miles from Liverpool, is a large house standing in a park of some 2,500 acres. A section of the estate is now a wild life safari park, and in recent times other land has been sold off for building, allowing the city to encroach. But the house remains standing in grounds that are still extensive, and it is as important to Lancastrians, in its way, as is Buckingham Palace to Londoners.

In 1952 the present earl, Edward John Stanley, was thirty-four years old. He had served in the Grenadier Guards and reached the rank of major. In his civil capacity he was Lord Lieutenant and Custos Rotulorum of the County of Lancaster, President of the Rugby Football League and lately retired Commanding Officer of the King's Regiment, TA. Four years earlier he had married Lady Isabel Milles-Lade, daughter of the late Hon. Henry Milles-Lade and sister of the 4th Earl Sondes.

The couple lived graciously, as befitted their rank. They employed a comptroller, an agent and a considerable staff, including a butler, under-butler, valet, French chef, house-keepers, personal and other maids, footmen, ground staff, foresters and gamekeepers. The household was generally peaceful and well run.

Lord Derby had a busy official calendar, and on the evening of Thursday 19 October 1952 he was fulfilling a dinner engagement at Altcar, some sixteen miles from his home. Lady Derby dined alone, and as was usual she had dinner served in the Smoking-Room adjoining the First Library on the first floor of Knowsley Hall. The Smoking-Room was equipped as a lounge, with comfortable settees, a small dining-table and chairs, a writing-desk and a television set.

Television was then still in its infancy as a mass entertainment, and those lucky enough to possess a set watched the entire programme, evenings only, whenever they could. Lady Derby was no exception. She liked to watch it as she dined, and the set was placed conveniently within her view as she sat at table. Watching it, she was half turned away from the door.

Mid-way through the meal, the door from the First Library opened and a trainee footman, Harold Winstanley, aged nineteen, came in. Lady Derby had spoken to Winstanley shortly before – she had passed him in the ground floor corridor and said, 'Good evening' – but she was surprised and shocked to see him now. He had not been summoned and was therefore intruding. He was smoking a cigarette – extremely bad form in the circumstances. And, most disturbing of all, he was holding a sub-machine-gun.

'What do you want?' she asked him.

Winstanley ignored the question, aimed the gun at her and said, 'Get up.' She obeyed him, and when he added, 'Turn round,' she turned away from him and faced the television set.

There was scarcely time to wonder what possessed the young man. He fired several shots in a short burst, and Lady Derby fell to the floor. She was not injured fatally but one of the bullets had struck her in the neck, and she lay on the floor pretending to be unconscious or dead. The next few moments were filled with confusion. She heard other people coming into the room, a babble of voices – and more shots …

Knowsley Hall is not normally the source of much trouble or disturbance, and the officers on duty at Prescot police station must have been surprised when, about 8.35 p.m. that day, a telephone call came from the Hall asking for a policeman and an ambulance. No further information was given at that time.

Police Inspector Arthur Smithies Tyrer was on duty. He sent a police car immediately, and an ambulance was summoned. A short time later, when a little more was known about the incident, the police response was more impressive. All available wireless-equipped cars were directed to Knowsley Hall, together with mobile lighting equipment, walkie-talkie sets, police dogs and reinforcements from other divisions. The Chief Constable of Liverpool sent extra men, as did the Officer-in-Charge of troops at Harrington Barracks, Formby. Senior officers also attended, and the Chief Constable of Lancashire, away on duty at the Police College, Ryton-on-Dunsmore, made haste to return.

A great fuss. And no wonder.

Harold Winstanley had killed two people and injured two others, including Lady Derby. He was said to be running amok at the Hall, wantonly firing a sten-gun.

A number of witnesses described it as a sten-gun, and indeed the weapon had that general appearance, but it was not a sten, though just as deadly. Its history – for present purposes – had begun ten years earlier.

In 1942 the No. 4. Army Commando Unit was taking part in its third raid on the French city of Dieppe and Private Bernard Kenneth Davies, a native of Wallasey, Cheshire, was in the thick of it.

The standing instructions to British troops engaged in such a raid were that any captured enemy equipment should be brought back and handed in at unit headquarters. Private Davies took from a dead German a 9-mm machine pistol, known as a Schmeisser or 'German sten', together with about eight magazines, each containing thirty-two rounds of 9-mm ammunition. Instructions are made to be broken. Private Davies did not hand in the weapon as required: he kept it and in due course smuggled it back to the United Kingdom and took it to his father's house in Wallasey. He placed it in a tin trunk and left it there. The trunk was locked and his father did not know what was in it.

Davies was demobilized in April 1946, and in July of that year he took work as a driver with the Allied Control Commission in Germany. Returning to Britain in 1949, he married and went to live in Liverpool. Some time later he moved to 12 Birkenhead

Road, Hoylake, Wirral, where his wife was proprietress of the Rendezvous Café.

Approximately two years later, when Davies heard that his father's house was to be demolished, he went there and collected some of his belongings. Among them was the tin trunk – by now he had lost the key. He took the trunk, unopened, to the Rendezvous Café.

There was a second gun, one not directly involved in the Knowsley Hall shootings but instrumental in starting the Schmeisser off on its deadly course. This was a German automatic pistol with the name 'Mauser' stamped on it. It was purchased some time prior to June 1952 by Alan Russell Cullen of 37 Lee Road, Hoylake, Wirral. The vendor was an unknown man whom Cullen happened to meet in the Dee Hotel, West Kirkby, Cheshire. In spite of widespread enquiries, this man was never traced.

When interviewed after the killings, Cullen told the following story.

He was a fireman on the coasting vessel *Sprayville* and often at sea for some time. He had a general interest in guns and weaponry. On a visit to the Dee Hotel he got into conversation with a stranger and discovered that they shared the same interest. When the man told him he had a Mauser pistol for sale, Cullen agreed to buy it. He handed over £2 and received the Mauser, with about two dozen rounds of .32 ammunition.

In June or thereabouts, Cullen called at the Rendezvous Café at Hoylake and got into conversation with Bernard Kenneth Davies, a relative by marriage. The subject was guns. Cullen boasted of his new acquisition and Davies then remembered the Schmeisser in the tin trunk. He fetched the Schmeisser (he had to force the trunk open, presumably) and showed it to Cullen. In due course the two men agreed to a swap: Davies took the Mauser and ammunition and Cullen the Schmeisser, with between 200 and 300 rounds of 9-mm ammunition, contained in magazines. The 'German sten' was on its way.

Enter Harold Winstanley – or 'Harry' as he was known to Cullen and other associates.

Harold Winstanley was born at Liverpool on 8 January 1933. He was one of a large, mixed family. Both his parents had married twice, and he was the second child of the second marriage of both his mother and his father. His father died in 1934, and two years later his mother was admitted to the Whittingham County Mental Hospital, having been certified under the Lunacy Act.

From an early age, Winstanley was brought up in Fazakerley Cottage Homes, where he received a good education. In March 1948 he was transferred to the Liverpool Working Boys' Home and soon found work as a wine steward at the Royal Liverpool Golf Club.

On 21 August 1950, having volunteered, he joined the Scots Guards, but after serving for only one year he was discharged as permanently unfit, suffering from osteo-chondritis-dessicans, a disease of the bones. The disease had affected both his knees and troubled him from time to time. He was able to go back to his former employment but did not stay long. On 14 December 1951 he joined the staff of Lord and Lady Derby at Knowsley Hall as a trainee footman.

In general terms he seems to have got on well with the staff at Knowsley Hall. There was some history of fainting and collapsing – associated no doubt with his illness – but apart from that nothing in the way of trouble or disagreement between Winstanley and either his employers or his colleagues. These circumstances make it all the more puzzling that within ten months of taking up his new employment he should have acted the way he did.

But let us continue the story of the gun.

About 9 p.m. on Tuesday 7 October 1952, Alan Russell Cullen went again to the Rendezvous Café at Hoylake and there met Harry Winstanley. They knew each other very well. Cullen had made Winstanley's acquaintance some two years earlier, while he was working at the Royal Liverpool Golf Club, and they had met frequently at the Rendezvous and other places. After they had chatted for a while (this is Cullen's version), Winstanley asked Cullen if he knew anyone who had a gun for sale. He said he wanted it to shoot rabbits on the Knowsley Estate. Cullen said he had one 'like a Tommy-gun' and wasn't sure whether it was a sten or not. They haggled about it until Cullen agreed to let Winstanley have the gun for a new pair of sports trousers and £3 in money. He did not have the gun with him but would bring it to another meeting.

They met by arrangement at James Street railway station, Liverpool, about 5 p.m. on Wednesday 8 October. Cullen had previously placed the gun in a brown suitcase, together with a box containing about 300 rounds of ammunition, five or six magazines and a pull-through. He had left the suitcase in the left-luggage office. After talking for a while, Cullen and Winstanley went together to the left-luggage office, collected the suitcase and went to the gents' toilets, where the deal they had previously agreed was completed. The suitcase was not part of the deal. When Winstanley left the toilets, he was carrying the gun down the front of his mackintosh and the box of ammunition and sundries in his hand. The last Cullen saw of him, Winstanley was walking from James Street station into the street.

Alan Russell Cullen was an agent but by no means an accomplice – except in relation to the minor offences involved in illegal firearms dealing. If he had had the slightest idea of what was to occur the following day, it is inconceivable that he would ever have passed the gun to Winstanley. No doubt he supposed that the rabbits in Knowsley Park would have to watch out, but it is unlikely that he thought much else.

What was going on in Winstanley's mind? It seems so very unlikely that he would have gone to such trouble to obtain the gun for so mundane a purpose as to shoot rabbits – a purpose for which it was entirely unsuitable. Were the murders part of a preconceived plan? Did he set out from James Street station intent on committing them? In a later statement he said he did not, and there was no evidence to the contrary, but if that is so, it is hard to imagine why he needed the gun at all. One thing is not in doubt: by the evening of the following day he had caused both murder and mayhem at Knowsley Hall.

When Inspector Tyrer arrived at the Hall, the ambulance was just about to leave. Aboard it he saw William Sullivan, Lord Derby's valet, who had a bullet wound in his right hand. The police surgeon, Dr David Archibald Hunt, was already present. Christina Mary Campbell, the assistant housekeeper, came up to the inspector and told him she believed Winstanley was still somewhere inside the Hall, still carrying the gun. In order to get inside, the inspector had to break a glass door panel and release the lock. Then, accompanied by Dr Hunt and Police Sergeant Wilson, he went along the corridor and upstairs.

The door of the Smoking-Room was locked, but once they had announced themselves they were admitted by Elizabeth Doxford, Lady Derby's personal maid. They saw the body of Walter Stallard, the butler, lying beside the dining-table and close to the door of the First Library. Across the room, near the desk, lay the body of Douglas Stuart, the under-butler. Both had died of gunshot wounds and were so certified by Dr Hunt.

In line between the bodies, Lady Derby lay in the centre of the room on the floor, supported by cushions and attended by Elizabeth Doxford. She was conscious but bleeding badly, and when Dr Hunt saw the bullet entry wound in the back of her neck, he must have feared the worst. However, he arranged for her to be taken without delay to Liverpool Royal Infirmary, and there it was discovered that the bullet had exited under her left ear and by good fortune had missed all vital organs.

Inspector Tyrer locked the doors to the Smoking-Room and handed the keys to Detective Constable Halliwell, who was left on guard. He circulated an alert by radio to all adjoining police force areas, then commenced a search of the Hall and grounds. As more police and troops arrived, they were deployed in the search for Harold Winstanley.

In fact, Winstanley had already left the grounds. William Price, a gamekeeper, had seen him leaving by the Ormskirk Lodge gate about 9 p.m. and had said 'Good night' to him before riding away on his bicycle. Winstanley had appeared normal. Price had not noticed that he was carrying a gun.

During the ensuing search, PC Frederick Kershaw found an empty Schmeisser magazine on the estate road some thirty yards short of the Ormskirk Lodge gate, and Thomas McCombe, a forestry worker, found a second empty magazine a short distance away.

About 11.40 p.m. on the same day, Winstanley went to a telephone kiosk in North John Street, Liverpool, used the 999 system and was put through to the Liverpool City Police. He told PC Walter Egerton that he wanted to give himself up for the 'Knowsley job'.

Egerton knew at once what Winstanley meant. Together with Police Constables Gordon Mitchell and James William Donohue he went to North John Street and saw Winstanley waiting beside the telephone kiosk. To approach him must have seemed a hazardous enterprise, since the officers knew what had gone before, but they did approach him – and when he took the Schmeisser from under his coat, they seized him and disarmed him.

'All right. I'm Winstanley,' he said. 'I don't know why I did it. I don't know why I did it.'

The news of Winstanley's arrest was a signal for a general easing of tension and a return to normal duties for many engaged in the search. Lady Derby, though detained in hospital, was doing well, and Lord Derby was with her. The valet, William Sullivan, had been treated for a flesh wound and discharged from hospital. The time-honoured process of informing the coroner, arranging the removal of the bodies to the mortuary and expert examination of the scene was well under way. Detective Chief Inspector W.A. Roberts and Detective Inspector Horace Teasdale, (both to be chief superintendents in due course) went to the Liverpool City Police Office and spoke to Winstanley.

After cautioning him, Roberts said, 'We are taking you to Prescot Police Station, as we believe you have been concerned in a shooting incident at Knowsley Hall.'

'All right,' he told them.

Winstanley was lodged in a cell at Prescot, and at 2.25 a.m. on Friday 10 October the two officers interviewed him again.

Roberts showed him the Schmeisser and said: 'Whilst you have been detained here we have been to Knowsley Hall and in the Smoking-Room have seen the dead bodies of Walter Stallard and Douglas Stuart. I have reason to believe that you caused their deaths by shooting them with this gun.'

'That's the gun all right,' he told them, adding in evident surprise, 'Oh. Isn't Lady Derby dead too?'

They explained that only the two men were dead and that Lady Derby had been injured and was in hospital.

'I know I shot her as well,' he said.

Winstanley was in no mood to conceal anything and made a statement under caution that amounted to a full confession. When he was charged with the murders, he said: 'I have told the truth in my statement. I did shoot Mr Walter Stallard. I did shoot Mr Douglas Stuart.'

So far, the pattern of events on the fateful night have been treated skimpily. Of course, the picture was more clear by this time, and many witnesses had been able to describe stages of the incident. But there can hardly be a clearer account than that of Winstanley himself – or a more chilling description than the words of his statement, as dictated to Horace Teasdale.

I have worked at Knowsley Hall since December and I have been treated well by Lord and Lady Derby and all the staff and I have no reason to do anybody any harm.

[He describes the meeting in Liverpool with 'a lad I know' (Cullen) and the transaction in which he obtained the Schmeisser.]

I put the gun down my trousers on the inside and the butt under my arm under my jacket. The ammunition, pull-through and magazines were in a cardboard box and I carried it in my hand …

I left him then and came back to Knowsley. It was nearly quarter to seven when I got back and I put it straight in the drawer in my room. After supper I loaded the magazine because all the bullets were loose. There was only about two hundred bullets altogether. Around ten o'clock I took the gun out and showed it to Terence Cooke [a steward]. I had put a magazine on before that and had been out in the grounds and had fired a few shots in the air, but nobody knew. When Terence saw the gun he said he didn't want anything to do with it and if he was me he'd get rid of it soon. I put the whole lot away then, in my drawer again. I got the gun out again on Thursday after lunch and stripped it all on my bed. I gave it all a good cleaning and oiling. Tried the magazines on to see that they fitted properly. They were empty then. I had emptied them …

During the afternoon … about ten past four … I showed Ann [Anne Mitchell, housemaid] one of the girls at the Hall, two of the bullets I had in my pocket and asked her if she would like one. She said, 'I don't like anybody messing around with bullets or guns.' I said, 'How would you like to see the real thing?' We were in the Stewards' Room then and I ran along to my room, got the gun, put the safety catch on and the magazine which was full. I should have told you that I had filled all the magazines again after cleaning the gun. I covered the gun with my mack and took it back to show Ann – She said the same thing again.

Someone came in then and I put it under the table. After that I didn't put it back in my room. I put it in the Stewards' Room pantry in a drawer. I didn't touch it again until after supper, that would be about quarter past eight. We all knew that Lord Derby had gone out for dinner but I knew Lady Derby was in. I got the gun out. It had one magazine on and I forgot to tell you that I had left a spare full magazine in the drawer with it after I had shown Ann. The safety catch was off and I went upstairs to the Smoking-Room where Lady Derby was having dinner.

I opened the door of the First Library and walked through and tapped lightly on the Smoking-Room door. I could hear that the television was on and I opened the door and walked in. Lady Derby was sitting down at the table having her dinner facing the television. She half turned round and she saw me. I raised the gun. She stood up and said, 'I'll tell you something,' or something like that. When I first went in the room I meant to ask Lady Derby to help me get rid of the gun, but when she looked at me I was frightened. I said to her, 'Turn round,' because I didn't want to shoot her when she was looking at me. As she turned towards the television I pulled the trigger and the bullets must have hit her as she fell down and moaned something. She looked dead to me and I went out into the First Library then.

Then Mr Stallard came and went into the Smoking-Room where Lady Derby was. I followed just into the room. He looked at Her Ladyship first and then at me. I got scared and pulled the trigger and fired a burst at him. He flopped down and looked dead to me. I went out again and closed the door. Then Douglas Stuart came and said, 'What's the noise?' I said, 'Mr Stallard has had an accident.' He went into the room and looked at Mr Stallard and Her Ladyship. I had the gun pointed from the hip at him and he said, 'I'll do anything for you and I'll not tell anybody what I've seen.' He crouched down behind the settee and I pulled the trigger and a few bullets came out. They didn't hit him because he got up and went to the other doorway. He was scared and said, 'My wife! My wife!' I said, 'I'll look after your wife.' I pulled on the trigger again and gave him I think two short bursts. He fell down and stopped there against the door.

I left the Smoking-Room and went into the hall where I saw William [Sullivan] His Lordship's valet, half-way down the stairs. He said, 'What's all the noise and what have you got that Sten gun for?' I then saw Iris [Caine, housemaid] and Ann on the landing. I said to William, 'I want to tell you something.' I waved to the girls to come down and said, 'I'm not going to do anything to you.' The girls would not come down and William dashed to the garden door and went down the stone steps. I ran after him and fired two short bursts at him. He would be about fifteen yards away from me and was turning into the liftway when I fired. I saw the wood splinter. I saw Mrs Turley [housekeeper] and Ena [maid] run into the passage. The gun was empty then and I put the safety catch on. I saw William sitting on the floor with his arm out and some blood and I could see I had wounded him. Iris and Ann and Miss Doxford came out of the liftway and I threatened I would shoot if they moved. Mrs Turley put her hand on my shoulder and said, 'Come on, Harry. What's wrong?' and offered to give me a cup of tea. I turned to Miss Doxford and said, 'I think I have killed Her Ladyship, Mr Stallard and Douglas.' The chef [Paul Dupuy] was running up the passage and I said, 'I'm not going to harm anybody,' and told him to go back.

I went to my room, put a full magazine on the gun and put all the other bullets I had in my pockets. I then went into the toilet and saw Mr Duggan [watchman] and a few other men there. Mr Duggan told me to put the gun down and not to be soft. The safety catch was on but I said, 'Don't come any further or I'll shoot.' I went out of the toilet and took the safety catch off and walked along the passage when the chef got hold of me and tried to take the gun off me. I transferred the gun to my left hand and pushed the chef. We both fell to the ground, me on top. I hit him with my right hand, and the gun went off with a short burst, and then I think it jammed.

I went out of the house then and towards Ormskirk Lodge and then took the jammed magazine out and put the magazine in my pocket and emptied another full one. I put the bullets in my pocket and threw that magazine away near Mr Wilcock's house. I put the gun down my trousers with the safety catch on and no magazine in it. I went to the Coppull House Inn, had a pint of beer, bought a bottle of beer and some crisps and took them out with me. I then made my way to a barn and made my mind up to give myself up as I knew it would be worse for me in the end. I went on a bus to North John Street, Liverpool, and phoned 999 from a kiosk.

He then describes the arrival of the police and his arrest and finishes off the statement: 'I know I've done wrong and I want to say I'm really sorry, but the real cause of it, I think, was panic.'

If an expert collator had set out to produce a summary of all the witness evidence, he could hardly have improved on that statement by Winstanley. One or two discrepancies were found, but they were quite minor, such as might have been expected in view of the prevailing confusion. Anne Mitchell and Terence Edward Cook agreed that they had been shown the gun and had advised Winstanley to get rid of it. Paul Dupuy, the French chef, had indeed tried to take the gun from him and had been struck for his pains. Robert Duggan, the watchman, and others said they had tried to persuade Winstanley to 'put up' the gun, and Duggan had climbed out through a toilet window to raise the alarm.

Perhaps the most remarkable evidence to come generally from the witnesses was their liking for Winstanley. He was 'a nice boy', 'jolly', 'an excellent type of youth', 'amiable', 'honest', 'kindly' and 'easy to get on with'. But the facts – and the supporting scientific evidence – left no doubt that he had been none of those things on the fateful night.

After several remands at Prescot Magistrates' Court, Winstanley was brought to trial at Manchester Assizes on 16 December 1952, before Mr Justice Jones. He entered a plea of 'Not guilty', a mere formality in the circumstances. Mr H.I. Nelson QC and Mr R.S. Nicklin appeared for the Crown, whilst

Winstanley was represented by Miss Rose Heilbron (later Mrs Justice Heilbron).

It was plain from the outset that counsel on both sides were in close accord in their views on Winstanley's condition. Opening the case for the prosecution, Mr Nelson QC went straight to the nub of the matter by saying that there was doubt about Winstanley's fitness to plead. But it was for the defence to prove unfitness, he said, and he proceeded to call his witnesses.

Lady Derby, recovered by now, gave evidence for eight minutes.

Cross-examination was not severe and seemed designed to elicit information about the state of Winstanley's mind. 'He was most obliging and helpful in every way,' said Christina Mary Campbell, the assistant housekeeper, 'but later, when he had the gun, his eyes were rather queer and staring.'

Miss Heilbron: 'Rather a mad look?'
Witness: 'Yes.'

In response to a question from Miss Heilbron, Detective Inspector Teasdale said, 'Since 5 August 1936, Winstanley's mother has been in Whittingham Mental Hospital. She is a schizophrenic case, living in a world of fantasy and devoid of reality.'

And so, according to the evidence at least, was Winstanley.

Opening the defence case, Miss Heilbron told the jury that the question at issue was not who had committed the crimes but whether Winstanley was responsible for his actions. She went on to call only one defence witness, Dr Francis Herbert Brisby, Senior Medical Officer of Walton Prison, Liverpool.

Dr Brisby had carried out observations on Winstanley whilst he had been in custody awaiting trial. He described some very curious behaviour on Winstanley's part, with attendant symptoms. He complained of spots and colours before the eyes and suffered physical collapse and mental confusion. Given a cigarette, he had not known what to do with it and had let it fall from his fingers. He was prone to falling suddenly asleep whilst obviously confused and would appear normal on waking. During these bouts of insensibility it had been possible to jab him with a pin without response.

Summarizing, the doctor told the jury that Winstanley was

suffering from schizophrenia and gross hysteria and would not be able to differentiate between right and wrong.

There was no conflict of evidence. The jury gave their verdict without retiring. On the charge of murdering Walter Stallard, Winstanley was found guilty but insane. By order of Mr Justice Jones, the remaining charges were not proceeded with.

Winstanley was ordered to be detained at Broadmoor 'until Her Majesty's pleasure be known'.

And what of Bernard Kenneth Davies and Alan Russell Cullen, amateur firearms dealers and previous owners of the Schmeisser gun and Mauser pistol? Both were prosecuted amid no great glare of publicity.

The Mauser was handed to police by Davies when they went to interview him. 'I have tried to be as co-operative as I can in this matter,' he told them. 'I would like to add that when I found out what had happened with the Schmeisser gun I left the Mauser pistol at home and instructed my wife that if the police called in my absence she was to hand the pistol to them.'

He had previously disposed of the Mauser ammunition when his wife complained about his possessing such things.

'One night, about August, I dropped it into the River Mersey when I was crossing in a ferry boat. I kept the pistol because I am in the Royal Marines Voluntary Reserve and I thought it would be useful in that connection.'

Davies was brought before Birkenhead County Magistrates' Court on 22 January 1953, summonsed for four offences of possessing and transferring firearms without the appropriate authorities and documents, under the Firearms Act, 1937. He was fined £5 in each case and allowed seven days in which to pay.

It does not seem a lot, but no doubt it sounded rather more stringent in 1952, when the pound was worth a deal more than now.

Cullen, it transpired, had not given all the ammunition to Winstanley. When his house was searched, two boxes of 9-mm ammunition were found and taken by the police.

He appeared before different magistrates – at Bromborough, Cheshire – on a much later date, 1 June 1953. The delay was due to his having been away at sea. By the time his case came up, the going rate had evidently risen. On five summonses for like offences he was fined £10 in each case and allowed to pay at the rate of £2 a week.

The guns and ammunition were ordered to be confiscated.

10 Never Talk to Strangers, Huyton 1963

Murder in fiction is invariably a complicated business involving many suspects, a sprinkling of red herrings and a lot of smart detective work before the culprit is unmasked. This can also be true of real-life cases, but often the truth is easier to find, the mystery less baffling. Yet such murders cannot always be dismissed as dull and undemanding.

The story of the murder of Paula Louisa Atkinson by Thomas Johnston is a simple one, soon uncovered, quickly detected and finally resolved with little publicity and no great battle of legal minds. But it is a cautionary tale, included here because it exemplifies the sort of danger we have in mind when we warn our children never to talk to strangers. Parents are well advised to read and consider it – as are shopkeepers and people who observe children at play – for a chance encounter between a child and a stranger may signal the beginning of a horrifying episode such as this.

Paula Louisa Atkinson was just three years old, daughter of Thomas Atkinson, a cable-maker, and Elizabeth Atkinson, of 17 Parbrook Close, Huyton, which is part of a corporation housing estate. A little after 6 p.m. on Friday 8 November 1963, she took her spending-money and went with her older sister to the shop at 121 Hillside Avenue, Huyton, a short distance from her home. The two little girls were served by shop assistant Mrs Wilma O'Reilly. But decisions about what to buy do not come easily. The children needed time to make up their minds. There was a man in the shop at the time, wanting cigarettes, and Mrs O'Reilly served him.

For some unexplained reason, Paula's sister left the shop first, a few minutes ahead of Paula. The other customer also left before she did. As Paula was leaving the shop, clutching an ice-cream, Mrs O'Reilly wisely advised her to 'Go straight home.'

Wisely, yes, but, to her later regret, not effectively.

A short time afterwards, children playing in the street noticed a man carrying a small child towards a piece of spare land lying between Endmoor Road and Stockbridge Road. They thought nothing of it at the time, and who can blame them? What could look more natural than a father carrying his child?

About 7.15 that evening, whilst walking on a footpath across the spare land, eighteen-year-old Frank Currie found the body of Paula Atkinson lying on a patch of muddy grass close to the path. He could see that her throat had been cut. Currie must have been shocked, but he had enough sense to leave the body where it lay and to inform the police.

Although the machinery of a murder investigation was put in motion at once – preservation of the scene, house-to-house enquiries, expert examination of the body and so on – it is fair to say that Thomas Johnston was the sole suspect almost from the start. His parental home was in the same district, at 38 Rosebank Road, Huyton, and he had a known propensity for sexual attacks on children. Moreover, that very day he had been listed as having absconded from Rainhill Mental Institution.

Johnston was then forty years of age, the fourth of six children, and had been born at Liverpool on 23 October 1923. Described as 'unemployed', he had actually done little work of any sort since leaving school at the age of twelve – a few weeks as a farm labourer, a few more as a dairy hand. He had joined the Army but was discharged as Grade 4 after only two weeks – and in the space of that fortnight he had been absent without leave. No wonder the Army washed their hands of him.

As a 'juvenile' he had several times been in court for offences of theft and assault, and then, on 21 October 1941, he appeared at the Quarter Sessions at Liverpool on charges of housebreaking, canteen-breaking and larceny of a pedal cycle. He admitted twenty-two additional offences, and these were taken into consideration by the court in passing sentence. Johnston was declared to be feeble-minded and, under the provisions of the Mental Deficiency Act, 1913 (as amended), he was ordered to be detained in Brockhalls Mental Institution, Blackburn. Some time later he was transferred to the Moss Side Mental Institution at Maghull, on the outskirts of Liverpool.

On 14 September 1948 he escaped from Moss Side and a little over three months later, not having been recaptured, was discharged by operation of law. In simple terms, this means that the order under which he was confined had expired, and with it the power to retake him.

Johnston was not at large for long. On 26 April 1949 he appeared at Manchester Assizes on charges of (1) common assault and (2) indecent assault against a female.

Evidence was given that he had approached a ten-year-old girl and a younger boy who were picking flowers in a field and had lured them into a wood on the pretext of showing them some wonderful flowers. There, after making the girl sit down, he had first kissed and cuddled her and then interfered with her private parts. When the girl started to cry, he gripped her by the throat and told her to keep quiet. In that case he had left his victim badly distressed but otherwise unharmed.

On being convicted he was sentenced to serve three and two years imprisonment to run concurrently. However, a few weeks later he was transferred to Rampton Hospital under an order obtained by the prison authorities.

From then on, Johnston was an inmate of various mental institutions, but he absconded at every opportunity, remaining at large for short periods. The police at Huyton knew him well. Time and again they received fresh messages about him and had to go knocking on his door. But apart from one occasion when he had been found in possession of a knife, they had not found him troublesome or difficult to handle. In more recent times he had seemed settled and more trustworthy. He had been allowed frequent week-end leaves, unsupervised, and had shown no tendency to default. The police became used to seeing him at home from time to time and, apart from checking his pass, they left him alone.

But absconding was another matter, not to be taken lightly, and when the police were informed, they went in search of him. On visiting the home of Johnston's parents in Rosebank Road, Detective Chief Inspector Joe Hampton discovered that a back window had been broken. Johnston's hospital clothing had been left at the house, and he had evidently changed into ordinary clothes. The chief inspector took details of the missing clothing and circulated an amended description of the escapee to all forces. Joe Hampton had scarcely done so when he received more serious information and went to join Detective Sergeant Knowles, Police Sergeant Mack and Detective Constable Middleton on the spare land off Stockbridge Road where the dead body of Paula Atkinson was lying.

Within minutes the police were circulating another message, detailing the murder and naming Thomas Johnston as strongly suspected and wanted for interview in connection with it. This was actually done whilst the police surgeon, Dr Gottlieb, was still at the scene and before the Home Office Pathologist, Dr St Hill, arrived to examine the body *in situ*. The police had every reason to be confident they knew the murderer.

The coroner was informed, and in due course the body was removed to the mortuary for post-mortem examination. A great many enquiries were made in Huyton and beyond, but the single vital question was the same in every case: 'Have you seen Thomas Johnston?'

Sergeant John Alexander Rickart and Constable James Collins of Liverpool City Police were just two of a large number of officers who carried a description of the wanted man. At 3.55 a.m. on the following morning, Saturday 9 November, Collins was patrolling on the Pier Head at Liverpool when he saw a man who answered Johnston's description. After watching the man for a few minutes he passed a message by radio, and Sergeant Rickart went to join him at the Pier Head.

Collins still had the man under observation. He was pacing up and down and looking very agitated. The two officers went up to him and asked him his name. He said: 'Johnston.'

They told him they believed he had absconded from Rainhill Mental Institution, and his reply confirmed their suspicions.

'I've done something to a little girl,' he said.

Johnston was arrested and taken to the main Bridewell at Cheapside. On the way he told them, 'The blade is down a grid.'

At 4.30 a.m. he was seen at Liverpool by Detective Inspector Bainbridge of the Lancashire Constabulary. Bainbridge cautioned him and told him: 'I'm going to take you back to Huyton. I think you know why.'

Johnston replied, 'Yes, sir. It's about the little girl. She was coming out of the shop and I had this razor blade. I was really going to go home for a shave but I just picked her up and put the razor blade across her throat, sir.'

On the way back to Huyton, Johnston said, 'She said, "Hello, Dad," and she took my hand. If she hadn't have said that, it wouldn't have happened.' And at a later stage of the journey he added, 'I threw the razor blade down a grid. I can show you where.' When they came to Huyton, he directed Inspector Bainbridge to drive down Stockbridge Road and into Melbury Road, where he pointed out a road-drainage grid. Subsequently, by using an electro-magnet, the police recovered an Ever Ready single-edged blade from the grid.

Only a few gaps remain in the story, and perhaps the best way to fill them is to consider the voluntary statement Johnston later made to Detective Chief Inspector Joe Hampton.

About twenty to twelve today [in fact, he meant the previous day, Friday] I went to the hospital canteen for a cup of tea. I was with a parole patient. I had to get rid of him, so I said, 'You go to the library. I'm going to the lavatory. I'll follow on.' When he had gone I ran away. I walked to Prescot, got a 10C bus and went home. The woman next door saw me and said, 'Your mother's gone out, Tommy.' As soon as she went in, I broke the window with a brick, opened the door and went in. I went in and changed into a fresh vest, shirt, trousers, pullover and shoes. I took five shillings from my money box and then broke into the meter and took the money out. I took my father's overcoat. Then I got the bus to the other side of Page Moss. I went to the pictures in Liverpool. It cost three and sixpence. I left there about five o'clock and went to the pub facing the Majestic Picture House. I bought a bottle of Guinness and came out. Then I said, 'I'll buy a razor blade, so I can go home and have a shave.' I asked for a one-sided razor blade and bought an Ever Ready for sixpence.

I stood in the bus queue for ten or twelve minutes and caught a bus to the Eagle and Child at Huyton. I went in a shop to buy ten woodbines. There was a little girl in there with an ice-cream in her hand. The lady in the shop told her, 'Go straight home.' She walked out behind me. She said, 'Hello, Dad,' and put her hand in my hand. So I turned right into a Close and I picked her up in my arms and there was some more kids playing about in the street but they didn't seem to take any notice of me carrying the baby. So I went over the bridge and down to the Alt [River Alt] and sat on the grass by a heap of soil.

So I started kissing her and she started screaming out then. So I went all nervous and I pulled out the razor blade and I went into a panic and I put the razor blade across her throat. She screamed again and I cut my finger with the blade and I put the blade in my top pocket in my jacket.

Then I run across the field to the telephone in Stockbridge Road. I went about a hundred yards down the road on the left, and I thought on about the blade then, so I took it out of my pocket and there was a mobile carrier what sells cigarettes, so I dropped the blade down the grid.

Then I went to Stockbridge Road again and got the bus and went to Liverpool. To Seacombe – over the water. And I went in a Chinese café and ordered steak, onions, sausage and chips and three cups of tea, and gave the girl a shilling tip. I put sixpence in the juke-box and had the Beatles on. I stayed there till it shut at half past eleven. Then I got the last boat across to Liverpool and then I went to a small open air café at the Pier Head and got a couple of cups of tea and I hanged about there for two or three hours or more. The police came looking round every so often, but they took no notice of me at first. It must have been about four o'clock and they came across and they'd seen me walking up and down …

The statement concluded with an account of his arrest by Sergeant Rickart and Constable Collins. He described it in almost exactly the words the officers had used.

The statement was easily verified. Johnston had bus tickets in his pocket for the journeys he had mentioned, and a number of witnesses were found who remembered seeing or speaking to him.

When Johnston was cautioned and charged with the wilful murder of Paula Louisa Atkinson, he wrote on the charge form:

'That's true, sir.'

On Wednesday 29 January 1964, following remands and committal at Prescot Magistrates' Court, Johnston appeared for trial at Liverpool Crown Court, before Mr Justice Melford Stevenson. Rose Heilbron QC (later Mrs Justice Heilbron) and Mr R.R. Leech appeared for the Crown, and Mr F.J. Nance for the defence.

The hearing never developed into a trial in the accepted sense. Miss Heilbron called only one witness for the prosecution and the defence none at all. In view of what the single witness had to say, a defence was hardly necessary

He was Dr William Stevens, Principal Medical Officer of Walton Prison, who had examined Johnston whilst he was in the prison awaiting trial. After detailing Johnston's mental history, he outlined the results of his own observations over a period and concluded by saying: 'Johnston suffers from hallucinations and is quite incapable of instructing counsel or of understanding the evidence.'

The jury had no difficulty in finding Johnston insane and unfit to plead to the charge. Mr Justice Melford Stevenson ordered him to be detained during Her Majesty's pleasure.

Following the trial, the Secretary of State at the Home Office directed, by warrant under Section 71 (2) of the Mental Health Act, 1959, that Johnston be detained at Rampton Hospital.

But as we know, he had been there before.

11 Too Many Hairs, Blackburn 1876

Or 'Hanged by a Hair' to give this sordid story a secondary title, as they used to in the old days.

The way in which the vital clue falls into place is all too familiar. The victim is a ravishing blonde – or a redhead, it's all the same – and the prime suspect denies ever having been in her company. But the astute detective notices a single blonde hair – or black, or grey, as the case may be – adhering to the suspect's sleeve, and when this is microscopically compared with a hair from the head of the victim, lo and behold, they match exactly and a confession follows.

The murder of Emily Mary Holland at Blackburn in 1876 was nothing like that. There were far too many hairs.

The crime itself, though atrocious and horrifying, was simple enough.

Emily Holland was seven years old, daughter of James Holland, a mechanic, of 110 Moss Street, Blackburn. On Tuesday 28 March 1876 she came home from school at the usual time and went to play in the street. When the time came for her to appear indoors, Emily was nowhere to be found. Her parents, no doubt annoyed at first, called at the homes of several of her friends, and it was some time later before they began to be alarmed. James Holland then went to Blackburn police station to report his daughter missing from home, and a search of the area commenced.

An hour is a long time when a young child is missing, but hope continues for a while longer. Even after a cold March night has elapsed there is still a chance that the child may be found unharmed. But after another day and another night, even the most optimistic of searchers begins to fear the worst. Emily's parents became distraught and, as the police continued the search, they arranged to have posters printed, urging the public to assist.

On Thursday 30 March, two days after Emily's disappearance, Mrs Alice White, of 73 Bastwell Terrace, Blackburn, was approached by a neighbour's child and invited to look at 'a parcel' in the field adjoining the terrace. Mrs White followed the child and saw something wrapped in newspapers. When she opened the parcel, she had the shock of her life. It contained the headless and limbless torso of a young girl. The torso was naked.

The Blackburn police were informed and took charge. The officers who went to the scene must have suspected from the outset that these were the remains of Emily Mary Holland, particularly since no other child was known to be missing, but a torso is anonymous, and they could only extend the search in the hope of finding the missing parts of the body.

A man called Richard Fairclough made the next discovery. He had noticed a man, carrying some kind of parcel, walking to and fro in an agitated way along a minor road at Lower Cunliffe, in the township of Rishton, more than a mile from Blackburn. The man eventually left the scene and, moved by curiosity, Fairclough scouted the area. He soon noticed a parcel, wrapped in newspaper, lying in a sough (drainage ditch) beside the road. Fairclough was not bold enough to open it, but he informed the police at Rishton, and Police Constable Riley went to investigate. The parcel contained two severed legs, and in due course they were shown to match the torso found earlier.

The description of the man, as supplied by Richard Fairclough to PC Riley, was inconclusive, as such descriptions frequently are, but the parcel was to yield valuable information later.

Somewhere in the area, it was supposed, must lie a third parcel containing the missing arms and head, but a prolonged search failed to locate it. Nevertheless, the police were now convinced the search for Mary Holland was over. When an inquest of identification was held the following day, all doubts were removed: Emily's mother positively identified the child by means of a familiar mark on her back.

Dr William Martland, police surgeon, of Blackburn, was called to examine the two parcels. He had already been told that PC Riley, in opening the parcel containing the legs, had seen a clump of loose hair enclosed with the limbs. He now noted that the legs and the torso were likewise covered with loose hairs which had adhered to blood smears and other moisture on the skin. The other moisture, he concluded at first, was due to the body having been wiped with a moist cloth, but he was to revise that view at a later stage.

The hairs interested him a great deal. There were so many and, assuming they were human hairs, it was clear they could not possibly all have come from the same person. They were of different lengths, different textures, different colours, coarse and fine, straight and curly, and all mingled in a puzzling tangle. A scientific gentleman by nature, Dr Martland leapt to an unscientific conclusion which proved in the end to be the correct one.

Where might so many different hairs be collected in one place?

Answer: In a barber's shop.

In the consultation that followed, something else was discussed and agreed. There is an affinity between barbers' shops and old newspapers. All barbers buy a few issues each day and distribute them on the premises for waiting customers to read.

When out of date they may be left to accumulate or used to wrap up sweepings from the shop floor. The newspapers used to make the two parcels all had one thing in common: they were issues of the *Preston Herald*, several of them in date order.

The inquest proper opened on Saturday 1 April 1876, at Blackburn Town Hall, before the borough coroner, Mr Hargreaves. It was adjourned until Friday 7 April, then further adjourned indefinitely, pending an investigation into the crime, although already, during the two hearings, some of the background story had begun to emerge.

On the day of her disappearance the dead girl had left school at 4 p.m. and in the course of the next hour was seen in Moss Street, close to her home, by two of her schoolmates.

Mary Ellen Eccles, aged eight, spoke to Emily, who told her a man had sent her to buy half an ounce of tobacco from Cox's shop. She had the money – 1½d – in her hand. Not long after,

Mary saw Emily talking to a man wearing a billy-cock hat, a brown suit and a yellow waistcoat. The description was not as distinctive as might be thought by today's observer: billy-cocks (rather resembling bowlers) were common wear at the time.

The other schoolmate was Jane Preston, aged nine. She also saw Emily Holland with a man. They were walking together along Moss Street. But Jane was not able to supply a useful description.

Several adult witnesses had seen Emily too, and they had seen a man, though not actually with the girl. A composite description was drawn up from all sources, and it became the target for officers on the enquiry. The shop proprietor, Mr Cox, had only seen Emily, but he confirmed her purchase of tobacco.

In addition to his evidence already mentioned, Dr Martland told the coroner and jury that the girl had been ravished and subjected to other forms of gross indecency.

During the five-day interval between the opening of the inquest and its further adjournment, a number of men answering the composite description were detained for questioning. All were released apart from one suspect. He was a tramp named Charles Taylor who had been begging in the Moss Street area about the time when Emily Holland was last seen alive. He had been seen by more than one witness, and in broad terms he fitted the description. That was enough to make Taylor a strong suspect for the murder.

Those five days were also a disturbing time for barbers in the town. Impressed by Dr Martland's conclusions, the police began a systematic search of all barbers' shops. The newspaper packaging and the untold hundreds of differing hairs carefully removed from the body had been packed off to a pathological laboratory at Liverpool for proper scientific examination, and the results would not be known for some time, but the Chief Constable, Mr Potts, was enthusiastic about the barber's shop theory and did not wait for official confirmation.

Two barbers had their shops actually in Moss Street, not far from Emily's home. It did not necessarily follow that one or other of these was the likeliest suspect, but both had the advantage of proximity, and Potts evidently thought that a good reason to go himself on the search of those two shops. In company with Superintendent Eastwood and others, he went on Monday 3 April to Denis Whitehead's shop, where a search revealed nothing. They went on to the shop of William Fish at 3 Moss Street.

This was a type of building common throughout the land: a shop on the ground floor with living-accommodation above. However, Fish had moved out some time previously and now lived with his family at 162 Moss Street. He still worked in the shop but used the upper rooms only for storing jumble.

Fish stood by while the officers searched his premises and did not object to a search of his clothing and himself. No traces of blood or signs of a struggle were found. However, one significant discovery was made. In the shop was a pile of old and recent copies of the *Preston Herald*. The issues of 11, 18 and 25 March 1876 and an issue for November 1875 were missing from the pile. These dates were the same as those on the newspapers used to wrap the torso and the severed legs.

Viewed in retrospect, this seems to have been strong enough circumstantial evidence to justify the detention and close questioning of Fish. The police of the time did not think so. Or perhaps they had other reasons for not taking action at that stage? Considering the nature of the crime, one can imagine that they had come to an obvious conclusion – that the killing and dissection had taken place somewhere indoors and that when they located the spot they would find heavy blood-staining. No such staining was found at 3 Moss Street. Therefore, to adapt a metaphor, the iron was not yet hot enough for striking.

The chief constable and the superintendent withdrew from the shop, leaving Police Constables Holden and Seward to sift through a pile of coals in the cellar. Presumably they searched properly. At any rate, they reported having found nothing of significance among the coals.

At the resumed inquest on Friday 7 April Dr Martland reported the result of a post-mortem examination on the remains, carried out by himself in the presence of Drs Cheeseborough and Patchett. The cause of death, he said, was partial suffocation followed by loss of blood from cutting of the throat. Dismembering had taken place up to two hours after death. His evidence was corroborated by his two colleagues.

Chief Constable Potts told the inquest about the many enquiries his men had made to date and referred to the arrest of the tramp, Charles Taylor, who was still in custody. Taylor, he said, had freely admitted begging in Moss Street on the afternoon of 28 March but continued to deny all knowledge of the murder, and since no fresh evidence had been found to incriminate him, Potts had concluded that Taylor was not the man responsible and now proposed to discharge him. The coroner concurred and Taylor was formally set free to return to his wandering.

Whether at that stage Potts mentioned his suspicion of William Fish is not recorded, but it cannot be doubted that such suspicion was being entertained. Ever since the search of his shop, Fish had been under constant police surveillance. And yet, if events mean anything, he was not the only suspect, for a similar watch was kept on the shop and movements of the other Moss Street barber, Denis Whitehead.

Neither man gave anything away by his actions. Whitehead did business as usual. Fish went to his shop every day, shaved his customers until closing time, then locked up and went home.

But if the police could not make up their minds, it seems the public could. Rumours sprang up and spread all over town. It is said that local children would gather round Fish as he sat on the shop doorstep puffing at his pipe and taunt him with chants of 'Barber. Who killed the girl?' and 'Emily, Emily, who murdered Emily?' Another report suggests that his business boomed, swelled by customers who had heard the rumours, half-believed them and went to gratify their morbid curiosity – and perhaps even to be shaved by the razor that had done the deed.

How much of this is myth, how much truth, is open to conjecture, but it is on record that in the neighbourhood of Moss Street considerable hostility began to build up against William Fish, so much so that he was moved to seek police protection. This was supplied, and one wonders how the officers felt, standing guard on a man who many people felt should have been in custody. Allegations of unjustified inactivity on the part of the police were rife – and still Fish remained free.

When more than two weeks had elapsed and the crime remained unsolved, a new line of enquiry was tried. Peter Taylor, of Preston, owned two dogs, a Clumber spaniel and a half-bred bloodhound named Morgan. (He said he owned them. In fact, the ownership of Morgan was disputed in a colourful exchange between Taylor and another man which was gleefully reported in the newspapers of the day – but this has no real bearing on the case.) Taylor called on Chief Constable Potts and offered the services of his dogs, which he said were good at following scents. Potts accepted the offer and detailed two detective officers, Livesey and Holden, to go with Taylor and search for the missing parts of the body. They searched from two starting-points: at Bastwell, where the torso had been found, and at Lower Cunliffe, scene of the discovery of the legs. The dogs searched well, so Taylor declared, and if they found nothing, that was because there was nothing there to be found.

Concealed officers were still watching the shops of Fish and Whitehead in Moss Street, and Chief Constable Potts, no doubt prompted by the availability of the dogs, decided to bring the vigil to an end. Late on the evening of Sunday 16 April, parties of searchers went simultaneously to the two shops. The respective owners were sent for and the shops entered. Then Taylor brought his dogs to each in turn, accompanied by the Chief Constable, Superintendent Eastwood and Detective Livesey. The dogs were first taken into Whitehead's shop but, though they searched it thoroughly, they found nothing incriminating.

On to the second shop, where Mr and Mrs Fish were waiting with PC Holden. If Fish was alarmed by the new development, he gave no sign of it. The search party went into the shop with Fish and his wife tailing behind.

When they were first released, the dogs spent some time downstairs, sniffing and searching with no apparent success. As Taylor said later, it was at the slopstone (sink) that they really started to work, and after that they showed sharp interest in the door that led upstairs. Taylor opened the door, and the dogs went up the stairs with a rush, the men and woman following. They sniffed in all corners of the back bedroom and among the piles of furniture and rubbish scattered on the floor. It seemed at first they would find nothing, but then both dogs dashed across the landing into the front bedroom – and what happened there must have been dramatic in the extreme.

The bloodhound made straight for the fireplace and stopped there with its head in the chimney cavity and its hair bristling with excitement.

'There's something up there,' Taylor said.

He pulled his dog away, reached an arm up the chimney and pulled down a bundle wrapped in newspaper. The newspaper was bloodstained and covered with loose hairs. When opened, it was found to contain the major part of a skull with tufts of hair attached, a number of pieces of bone broken from the skull, some smaller bones, evidently from the arms and hands of a child, and a few scraps of clothing of similar material to those Emily Holland had been wearing at the time of her disappearance. All the items were charred and blackened from burning.

It might be supposed that Fish was near to collapse and ready to confess when faced with this evidence, but he seems to have borne up well. He made no admissions when told he was being arrested for the murder of Emily Holland, and when, at Blackburn police station, he was cautioned and charged with the crime, his reply was: 'I am innocent, and God knows I am.'

It was reported at the time that news of the arrest spread quickly, and a large and hostile crowd gathered outside the Moss Street shop with the evident intention of venting their anger on Fish. This is said to have been thwarted by a police ruse. The Chief Constable addressed the crowd and told them frankly what had been found there – and whilst they attended the announcement with great interest, Fish was being whisked away by other officers along the back street.

Denial persisted and remorse was still absent when on the following morning Fish was arraigned before Blackburn Borough Magistrates' Court. Chief Constable Potts gave brief details of the discoveries at the shop and the arrest, and asked that Fish be remanded in custody. When asked by the magistrates if he had anything to say, Fish replied firmly: 'I know nothing about it. I am as innocent as a child.'

He was placed in the cells, and there he must have reviewed and revised his position, for later that afternoon he made a short verbal statement to PC William Parkinson. When Parkinson reported the conversation to his superiors, they went to see Fish, and with little persuasion he made the following written statement, which he signed.

I told Constable William Parkinson that I had burnt part of the clothes and put the other part under the coals in my shop. I now wish to say that I am guilty of the murder. I further wish to say that I do not want the innocent to suffer.

At a few minutes after five o'clock in the evening I was standing at my shop door in Moss Street when the deceased child came past. She was going up Moss Street. I asked her to bring me half an ounce of tobacco from Cox's shop. She went and brought it to me. I asked her to go into the shop. She did so. I asked her to go upstairs and she did. I went up with her. I tried to abuse her and she was nearly dead. I then cut her throat with a razor. This was in the front room, near the fire. I then carried the body downstairs into the shop, cut off the head, arms and legs, wrapped up the body in newspapers on the floor, wrapped up the legs also in newspapers and put the parcels into a box in the back kitchen. The arms and head I put into the fire.

On the Wednesday afternoon I took the parcel containing the legs to Lower Cunliffe and at nine o'clock that night I took the parcel containing the body to a field at Bastwell near Blackburn Cemetery and threw it over the wall. On Friday afternoon I burnt part of the clothing. On the Wednesday evening I took a part of the head which was unburnt and put it up the chimney in the front bedroom …

The statement ended: 'I further wish to say that I did it all myself. No other person had anything to do with it.'

Why Fish should say that is a mystery, and yet, in an earlier part of the statement, he had said, '… I do not want the innocent to suffer.' And in court at a later stage he again denied that any other man had been involved with him. All of this gives rise to the assumption that some other man was at least suspected. If it had been the other barber, Whitehead, that would explain why the police kept up their interest in both shops right up to the time of arrest. As we know too well, paedophiles do sometimes organize their activities, but I have found no evidence of a linked suspicion, and the thought of two barbers conspiring together to rape and murder a child seems unlikely. I much prefer Fish's version: 'I did it all myself.'

What sort of a man – or monster – was this William Fish? He

was twenty-six years old and has been variously described as poorly built and diminutive. He sported a slight moustache.

He was born in Darwen and brought up, presumably as an orphan, in the workhouse at Blackburn. Nothing is known of his parents or the circumstances in which he was placed in care. At the age of eleven he entered the hairdressing trade, being apprenticed to C.B. Barker at his shop in Northgate, Blackburn. Two years later he ran away but, after an unexplained three-year absence, returned, and Barker allowed the apprenticeship to continue. Around Christmas 1870, he was charged with stealing money from his employer and was sent to prison for fourteen days. Soon after his release he married and set up his own business in Moss Street.

A family man with two young children of his own, Fish hardly seemed the type to commit a murder of this sort. His motive can only have been sexually based – a common enough motive in all conscience for attacks of this kind.

The confession statement sparked off fresh activity.

On the following day, Monday 17 April, the police went again to Fish's shop to conduct a further search. The whole fireplace in the front bedroom was taken apart brick by brick, and more bones were found, also scraps of paper and clothing lodged in the draught hole. Among the bones were pieces of skull to which traces of brain tissue were still attached. More bones were found in a cigar box. And under the coals, where the police said they had searched earlier without success, they now found pieces of torn clothing which was later identified as having belonged to Emily Holland.

The police were severely criticized by the courts and the press for this apparent lapse. The accusation was also made that, if they had searched properly on their first visit, on 3 April, they would have found the parcel up the chimney and thus brought the case to an earlier conclusion. Of course, such things are easy to say with the benefit of hindsight, but perhaps they ought to have felt up the chimney, and certainly the coals might have been better searched – if they were searched at all. Defending the point, Chief Constable Potts said it should be remembered that on 3 April they were engaged in searching all barbers' shops in the town and had no evidence pointing particularly to Fish's shop.

A nice try, that, but I still can't help siding a little with the critics. No evidence against Fish? What about those missing newspapers whose dates accorded so precisely with those used to wrap up the dismembered body?

When the inquest on the girl was resumed, on Thursday 20 April, the jury had no lack of evidence satisfactorily to tie the loose ends of the case. They quickly returned a verdict of 'Wilful Murder' against William Fish. In due course he was committed for trial at the next assizes.

On Friday 28 July the trial began at Liverpool Assizes before Mr Justice Lindley. The prosecution was conducted by Mr Higgin QC and Mr Pope QC. On the direction of His Lordship (there being no cut-and-dried legal aid system in those days), Fish was represented by Mr Blair.

Among the witnesses called for the prosecution, by far the most important were the medical men. Dr Martland must have looked an impressive figure, standing in the witness box amid an array of boxes containing the exhibits. Skull and bits of skull, charred but still identifiable bones, pieces of charred and torn clothing belonging to Emily Holland: all these had their little parts of the story to tell. Fish's clothing was on display, together with roller towels from the shop, for scientific examination had revealed traces of blood on them. And of course the hairs: so many little slides, designed to show not comparison, as is usually the case, but great diversity.

After dealing again with his post-mortem findings, Dr Martland recounted an interview he had had with Fish. Fish had described how he fetched the razor from downstairs in order to cut the girl's throat. Later he had used the razor to shave 'a man from Birley Street'. And then the cutting-up of the body and the burning of some parts: Fish, he said, had agreed with all his findings except one. 'I did not wipe the body with a moist cloth, Doctor,' he had said. Dr Martland accepted Fish's version by revising his own. 'I said the body had been wiped over,' he told the court. 'Now I believe the girl had broken out into a cold sweat and the hairs were sticking to the sweat.'

Cross-examined by Blair, for Fish, Dr Martland said there were no signs of lunacy in Fish. This was corroborated by Drs Cheeseborough and Patchett.

Evidence of the grim discoveries was given by the various

witnesses. The dog-handler, Taylor, and the officers accompanying him described the search of the shop and Fish's arrest. Then the Chief Constable read Fish's confession to the court, and that must have made the jury's conclusion virtually foregone.

No witnesses were called for the defence, but Blair did his best to set up a defence of insanity. 'Fish must have been mad,' he said, 'to do such a thing. If you have any doubt that he was mentally disabled, give Fish the benefit of it.'

The judge referred to this in his summing-up, pointing out to the jury that the onus of proving the accused's insanity rested with the defence – and that they had not adduced any evidence to support it.

Without retiring, the jury returned a verdict of 'Guilty'.

Fish was clearly contrite and accepted the verdict without protest. When asked if there was any reason why sentence of death should not be passed, he said: 'My Lord and gentlemen of the jury: at the time I did the deed I did not know what I was doing. It came over me all at once. I never had such a thought in my head when I sent her for the tobacco.'

He was sentenced to die by hanging, and the sentence was carried out at Kirkdale Prison, Liverpool, on Monday 14 August 1876.

12   The Beerhouse Killing, Ribchester 1862

The Joiner's Arms at Ribchester was by no means the type of hostelry the name suggests. The only bar was a dining-table in Ann Walne's living-room, the only cellar a few wooden barrels kept under the table, and the only staff, Ann herself.

Ann Walne was born in 1783. She lived for seventy-nine years. And since at that age she was said to be strong and active, she might well have lived to be a hundred – if she had not been murdered.

In November 1862 she was a widow, living alone. Her husband had died seventeen years before, her daughter was married and living in the south. Her nearest living relative was her son, John Walne, who farmed at Hothersall, several miles away.

The best way to describe the Joiner's Arms is as a cottage with a smallholding attached. It stood in Fleet Lane, Ribchester, a mile or so on the Longridge side of the village. Ann had lived there for many years and earned her living from the produce of a few milking cows and the takings from her beerhouse.

One report suggests that she held a beer off-licence but, if that is true, both she and Joseph Ward, labour-master at the nearby Ribchester Workhouse, were in breach of the Beerhouses Act, 1834, when on the evening of 10 November 1862 Ward called at the house and quaffed a pint of best ale in her company.

Hardly an event worthy of comment, you think?

Perhaps so, on the face of it. Except that Joseph Ward was the last person, apart from her killers, to see Ann Walne alive. Ward was also the first to find her dead, but no significance should be read into the coincidence. Whoever killed her, it was not Joseph Ward.

Ribchester is a small but historic village nestling on the northern bank of Lancashire's River Ribble, with panoramic views of the surrounding hills. Once a Roman settlement stood there, and many relics of the Roman period are preserved in and behind a small museum overlooking the river. The village is popular with tourists and is considered by many to be the most picturesque in the Ribble Valley. Not the sort of place where you would expect to find ruffians or murderers – or a workhouse, for that matter.

But go back to the 1860s. The district was wilder then, the village more remote, and callers at Ann Walne's beerhouse were mainly local people. The only strangers among her customers were occasional travellers between Blackburn and Longridge or Preston.

Joseph Ward was more than a customer: he was a valued friend. He had known the old lady for many years. He called at her house for his pint of beer on most evenings – and of late, recognizing her need for help, he had taken to visiting the farm each morning to fodder and milk her cows. On the evening of 10 November he had left her hale and cheerful.

Early on the following day, when he arrived to tend her cattle, he found the cottage in darkness. This was unusual. Ann was an early riser and he had expected her to be about to greet him as she invariably was. But Ward was not worried unduly. She must have felt like a lie-in, he assumed. After tapping lightly on the door and receiving no response, he went about his work.

During the next hour and a half he knocked on her door a number of times, and when daylight came, he began to be worried. His alarm grew when he noticed that the front-door key was fitted in the lock – on the outside. After some hesitation, Ward unlocked the door and tried to open it, but the door would open only an inch or so and was obviously blocked by some obstruction. He went round to the back of the cottage and was shocked to find a gaping hole where the back window should have been. The entire frame, with protecting bars and securing stanchions, had been wrenched from the stonework and was lying on the ground.

At moments such as that, even the bravest among us feels alone, and understandably Ward was afraid to enter. He knew that in recent months there had been several robberies in the district. Perhaps the robbers were still in the cottage? Even worse, if he went in, he might find himself accused.

'I bethought myself of Bill Pye,' he explained later, 'and I went to fetch him.'

William Pye, a farmer in a bigger way of business, lived not far away. He went with Ward back to the cottage. They climbed in through the window space to find the downstairs rooms in confusion, with drawers flung out and contents scattered. A pile of chairs and other furniture had been used to barricade the front door on the inside. It was clear that a very rough burglary had been carried out.

That was bad of itself, but Ward and Pye were concerned about more than burglary. What had happened to Mrs Walne? They went somewhat fearfully upstairs to her bedroom and found her lying on the bed with arms outstretched and wrists tied to the bed-rail. She was shockingly injured and the lower part of her body was naked.

'I felt her thigh,' Ward said. 'She was dead enough.'

Even in those early days, Ribchester had its police house. The resident officer, Sergeant Whiteside, hurried to the cottage and beershop and joined the two men. Describing the scene at a later stage, he said: 'I noticed the clock had stopped at seventeen minutes past two. The clock case was standing open. Going upstairs I found the deceased tied to the bed by the wrists with cotton handkerchieves and lying on her back. The bedclothes were all tangled and thrown about. Her legs and thighs were bare. There was a pillow lying across her lower body and a bolster on her chest. Her face was covered with a woollen shawl. Two more handkerchieves were round her neck, one of them tied tightly. She had several wounds about the head and there was blood everywhere …'

I am sometimes suspicious of the evidence of stopped time-pieces, but this seems to have been a genuine case. As would be learned later, the clock case had been rummaged through in a search for money. The pendulum must have been halted in its course, and the clock would have stopped at that time. It is safe to assume that the approximate time of the murder was 2.17 a.m.

And continuing the theme of time, I have to admit feeling

sceptical on reading two related items in an old newspaper clipping describing the scene:

'The body was quite cold and it was evident that death had taken place some hours before ...'

'From a ghastly wound in the temple and another on the right ear, blood was slowly trickling, staining the bedclothes a deep red.'

Surely, I reasoned, when the heart stops beating, blood begins to drain from the higher organs and finds its lowest level. Bleeding ceases quite rapidly, and any blood remaining in the wounds congeals as the body cools.

But I soon had to revise my views.

During further research I came upon an official statement by Dr William Martland, police surgeon, (later to be instrumental in solving the William Fish case), who performed a post-mortem examination on 14 November – *four days* after the murder.

'At the time of the post mortem,' the doctor stated, 'blood was oozing from the ear ...'

Sergeant Whiteside seems to have been a capable man, but he knew murder was outside his scope. After making a preliminary examination, he went back to the village and used the magnetic telegraph to inform his superiors. On horseback to Ribchester came Superintendent McNab from Blackburn and Superintendent Green from Preston, both officers of the Lancashire County force. Together with Whiteside they made enquiries into the crime. An arrest was soon made – the wrong one, as it turned out.

Reading behind the words of later testimony, it was the sergeant who settled on Thomas Davis as the culprit. As the village 'bobby', it was part of his job to know everything that went on on his beat, including the tittle-tattle. He had heard local gossip suggesting that Davis and Mrs Walne were at loggerheads over some small matter, and he reasoned that the trouble must have come to a head between them and that Davis had killed the old woman out of spite. The assumption seems to have been made that robbery was not the motive, based on the discovery of a small amount of money in a dish beside the bed. Moreover, there were footprints in the vicinity of the cottage, some of which seemed to match boots Davis was wearing at the time. On this slender evidence, Thomas Davis was arrested and charged with murder.

But no more evidence against Davis was found, and what they had was not enough. When the inquest into the death was completed some weeks later – having been adjourned – the verdict of the coroner's jury did not support the police contention. Davis was present as the only suspect, to hear the jury declare that Ann Walne had been murdered by 'some person or persons unknown'.

When the inquest was over, Davis was taken briefly before a magistrate at Preston and discharged. He made a plea for pecuniary compensation but this was refused. There had been reasonable grounds for his arrest, he was told, and though his detention for so long a time was regrettable, it did not entitle him to be compensated. So Davis went free – and rightly so – but it can be imagined that he was rather disgruntled.

With Davis gone, the prospect for a detection must have seemed bleak. And so it was, until a reward of £100 was offered for information leading to the arrest and conviction of the killer. £100 was a fortune in those days, and it was not long before the police found a taker, one Thomas Bowling, known in the district as 'Chorley Tom'.

Something ought to be said about this individual. He was employed as a gamekeeper on an estate at Samlesbury, between Preston and Blackburn, but he also had convictions for poaching and had served several short terms of imprisonment. He had once been tried at Liverpool Assizes for maliciously shooting at another man but had been acquitted. He was strongly suspected of committing offences of burglary in the Blackburn area. And, if later accounts are to be believed, he was more closely involved in the Ribchester murder than he pretended.

In his bid for the reward, Chorley Tom named five men as being responsible for the crime. These were Duncan McPhail, Daniel Carr, Benjamin Hartley, George Woods and William Woods, younger brother of George. On Monday 1 December 1862 the five were arrested – and it seems Chorley Tom was arrested too. However, only the five were charged with murder, and when they were brought before Blackburn County Magistrates' Court for remand, the police stated they had 'accepted the evidence' of a sixth man – undoubtedly Chorley Tom Bowling. They were reluctant to say much more about the sixth man and claimed it would be against the interests of justice if the court enquired too deeply into the circumstances of his arrest.

The five were remanded to cells, and the police, who had nothing against them beyond the word of Chorley Tom, began to seek more evidence to strengthen their case. It was then that their hopes received a substantial boost. Superintendent Higgs, who had applied for the remand in custody, was told that Benjamin Hartley wanted to confess.

Hartley was taken from the cells to a private room, where he made a detailed statement on the following lines.

'I have known Dan Carr for many years,' he began, 'and Duncan McPhail since last Preston Guild.'

This, by the way, was not meant as a joke, though knowing readers might think it was. The Preston Guild – or, more properly, Guild Merchant – is a week-long festivity held in Preston by tradition every twenty years. Among Lancastrians, to say 'I haven't seen you since last Preston Guild' is to imply a very long period indeed. But Hartley was serious. There had been a Preston Guild in 1862, only a few months earlier, and he had met McPhail there, being introduced to him by Chorley Tom.

'About a week before the murder,' Hartley's statement went on, 'McPhail told me about an old woman who kept a beerhouse at Ribchester and had recently sold a cow to pay her rent. "The old lady's got the money by her and we must have it," McPhail said, adding that he was "fast" for money.'

The scheme had been ill fated from the beginning, Hartley explained. They had planned to go to Ribchester in McPhail's horse-drawn trap, starting from Salford Bridge (in Blackburn), and had met there on Saturday 8 November. But McPhail had been reluctant to use his conveyance, so they had postponed the plan. The next night, Sunday, they all met at Dan Carr's house but, because George Woods was very drunk, the plan was put off again until the following evening.

'McPhail came to my house about six o'clock on the Monday evening. He had a "dark" lantern with him. We set off together and met up with Carr and George Woods. We agreed to go to Ribchester on foot. We started from Salford Bridge and went up Penny Street, past the Bull's Head and the Bonny Inn and down Barker's Brow ...'

Here Hartley is describing giant strides. From Salford Bridge to the Bull's Head is well over a mile, the Bonny Inn as far again, and by the time they reached the foot of Barker's Brow they were half-way to Ribchester.

'George Woods had a crowbar and a stick. Dan Carr had a cane with a bit of copper wire attached and lead wrapped round the end. McPhail had a crowbar and a loaded pistol. I was not carrying any weapon. It was hailstoning: a rough, stormy night. On the way we met a man walking towards Blackburn and passed comment with him about the weather ...'

After they had crossed the river and before they reached the village, McPhail said he knew of a path through the fields that passed the old woman's house. 'It will be the quietest way,' he said. They followed the path and came at length to an isolated barn. McPhail used the crowbar to break the staple off the door, and they went inside. They lay on the hay near some cows, and McPhail and Carr produced flasks of rum which they passed round. When the rum was gone, they went on and came to Ann Walne's beerhouse. They spent some time in one of her outhouses, then McPhail said it was time to begin.

They told me to stand at the end of the house and see if anybody came up the lane and they would go and examine the window. Shortly afterwards, McPhail came back and said, 'They have got the window out. In with you.'

George Woods went in first and I followed him. Then Carr and McPhail. Carr struck a match and lighted the 'dark' lantern and gave it to George Woods.

George and I went upstairs and saw the old woman sitting up in bed. George asked her, 'Where is your money?' She started screaming so I held her down on her back while George was rooting about in the bed. We both went downstairs and Dan Carr and McPhail were searching the cupboards and looking in the clock, using a candle. The old woman was still screaming so I went upstairs again with George Woods and Carr. I held the woman down on the bed. Dan Carr said, 'I'll make her make less din,' and he took out the cane with the lead on the end and struck a blow at her head. I had my hand on her brow and the cane struck my hand. I thought he had broken my hand. I said, 'Oh dear. What art thou for?' He said, 'Did I hit thee, lad?' I said, 'Aye.' Then he struck the old woman twice on the side of her head and she shouted out, 'Oh dear. You have killed me.' George Woods was holding the light. We all went downstairs and left her alone. Dan Carr said, 'She must be tied, lads.' George Woods got some handkerchieves off the clothes maiden and he and I went upstairs. I said, 'George, you must tie her. I can't lift my hand.' So Woods used the handkerchieves to tie her hands to the bed-posts. While he was doing so, Carr and McPhail were upstairs, searching about. The old woman was alive when he tied her hands but she kept moaning.

When we had finished we all went out of the window and through the gateway to some cottages nearby, then up the lane to Longridge and on to Preston. Woods took the lead off his cane, put the lead in his pocket and threw the cane away. McPhail threw his crowbar away and passed the pistol to George Woods. When we were passing the railway near Preston, Woods told us he had got the money. He had it wrapped in a piece of flannel. He threw the flannel away and we divided the money. I got £4.10s.6d and the others got the same. When we got to Preston, McPhail and Woods went on to book at Bamber Bridge Station. I went to a pub in Preston with Dan Carr. Then we went to the railway station and got the 6 a.m. train back to Cherry Tree [a district near Blackburn].

The blow Dan Carr struck the old woman was a hard one and it made her head rattle.

One significant feature of Hartley's statement was the absence of any reference to William Woods, younger brother of George. Chorley Tom had named him as one of the gang, but it is virtually certain that he played no part. All the evidence pointed to a four-man gang, and the names of the four appeared consistently in Hartley's statement. Young Woods was later able to convince the magistrates and the police that he had been in Blackburn at the time of the murder. Nor was he an accessory, either before or after the fact, since he had never had cause to suspect that his brother or any of the others had taken part in the murder. The police offered no evidence against him, and the magistrates discharged him 'without a stain on his character'.

On Tuesday 2 December, the day after Hartley's confession, Superintendents Green and McNab met again at Ribchester, at the barn of William Duxbury, half a mile from Mrs Walne's beerhouse. The staple had been forced from the door as Hartley had described, and there were instrument marks on the timber. The floor of the barn was earthen and in places soft, and here and there in the softer places were marks of boots. They covered the best marks to protect them from damage by animals.

Two days later, this time accompanied by Hartley as their guide, the two officers surveyed the route followed by the gang in approaching the scene of the crime and leaving it in the Preston direction. Hartley pointed out to them the place where he said McPhail had thrown away his crowbar. It was still there, and they recovered it. Their search for a cane 'with a piece of copper wire attached' and the flannel used to wrap the stolen money was not successful. Both items, it transpired, had already been found and moved by other people and, following publicity, were later handed to the police.

On this visit the police had with them the boots of George Woods, Duncan McPhail and Daniel Carr. They used the boots to make impressions in the floor of the barn and compared them with the impressions they had earlier found and protected. In the cases of Carr and Woods – but not McPhail – they found exact comparisons. To achieve this piece of evidence they counted the nail patterns in both 'made' and 'found' marks and also used calipers to measure all the marks. Later the same day they had plaster casts taken of all the marks.

McPhail's crowbar was fitted into gouge marks on the barn door and similar marks in the back window frame of Mrs Walne's house. It was evident that all the marks had been made by the same crowbar.

Continuing their enquiries during the days that followed, the police found a number of independent witnesses who could confirm parts of the story told by Hartley.

The case against McPhail, George Woods, Carr and, of course, the informer, Benjamin Hartley, was now reasonably strong, and when next brought before the magistrates they were committed for trial at the next assizes. Hartley was dealt with at a separate hearing, his committal a formality, since no evidence would be offered against him in view of his co-operation.

Effectively, then, the tally of accused men had been reduced to three. In a development which could not have been foreseen, it was to be still further reduced only hours before the trial.

On the morning of Monday 30 March 1863, while being prepared by warders for the trial due that day, Daniel Carr was taken ill in his cell. It seemed a simple indisposition, a matter of coughing and gasping, and since he was known to suffer from an asthmatic condition it caused the warders no concern. However, when the coughing subsided, he failed to rise from his chair and had evidently collapsed. The prison doctor was sent for – and when he arrived only a few minutes later, he discovered that Carr was dead.

Thus the trial opened with only McPhail and Woods standing in the dock. His Lordship had been informed of the death of one prisoner and so was not surprised, but it is said that the surviving pair showed concern at Carr's absence and, not being informed of his death, were left wondering if he – like Hartley – had turned Queen's Evidence.

Frankly, I doubt the truth of that report. Certainly no public announcement was made of Carr's death until after the trial, but the defence lawyers must have known, and I feel they would have whispered the news to their clients.

The judge was Mr Baron Martin. Mr Higgin QC, Mr Kay and Mr Cottingham appeared for the prosecution. Woods was represented by Mr Pope, McPhail by Ernest Jones.

I have been unable to find any antecedents of George Woods, except that he was a joiner. Duncan McPhail, however, is known to have had a somewhat chequered career. He was forty years of age and married. His father had been resident minister of the Baptist chapel at Huncoat, near Accrington. McPhail had been in business as a tailor at Chorley until 1852, when, following conviction on seven charges of perjury, he was sentenced to transportation for seven years on each count, to run concurrently. In 1855 he obtained a 'Ticket of Leave' (parole repatriation) and returned to Blackburn, where he set up in business as a coal-dealer at Witton. When that business failed, he kept his pony and cart and began a new business as a hawker of cheese, bacon and other groceries. He was so employed up to the time of his arrest.

The trial lasted five days, and many witnesses were called to testify, of which the following is a selection.

G. Bower of the County Constabulary Office produced detailed plans of the murder scene and the route said to have been followed by the gang before and after the crime.

John Walne, farmer, of Hothersall, Longridge, identified the deceased as his mother and gave an account of her circumstances.

Joseph Ward, labour-master at Ribchester Workhouse, and William Pye, farmer, described finding the body.

Police Sergeant Whiteside detailed his observations when summoned to the beerhouse and the action he had taken.

In cross-examination, Whiteside was called to task about his arrest of the innocent Thomas Davis, and he justified it as best he could. He said: 'There are upwards of twenty paupers lodging in some cottages near deceased's house. Davis was one of them. I found some footmarks near the scene that matched his, and they went in the direction of the cottages. I believed they were Davis's footmarks. I interviewed Davis about the crime on three occasions. I do not know if Davis was ever an associate of Chorley Tom or of Benjamin Hartley.'

He was right about the footprints that 'went in the direction of the cottages'. As Hartley said in his statement, that was the direction in which the gang had quitted the scene.

Dr William Martland, the police surgeon, gave the result of his post-mortem examination of Mrs. Walne. Her left eye was swollen, and her nose crushed and broken. There were two other serious wounds on her face, caused in his opinion by some pointed instrument. And – as mentioned earlier – blood was still oozing from her ear. There was no evidence of a sexual attack.

Bad as the head wounds were (one of them had fractured her skull), they were not in his opinion the cause of death. The cause, he said, was suffocation resulting from the woollen shawl over her face which had at one stage been forced into her mouth. Dr Martland also said he had examined the left hand of Benjamin Hartley and had found a large bruise on it, consistent with a heavy blow from some instrument.

William Sharples, a bobbin-turner of Ribchester, had seen McPhail unreining his horse outside the Joiner's Arms about a week before the murder. 'I have seen him there before,' Sharples deposed. 'I know him well enough. He goes about with a pony and cart, selling bacon and cheese.'

Joseph Molyneux, a weaver of Grimsargh, was passing the Grimsargh police station early on the morning of Tuesday 11 November 1862 when he saw four sets of footprints in recently fallen snow. 'They were shoes, not clogs,' he said, 'and they were pointing in the direction of Preston.'

James Nixon, a greengrocer of Blackburn, said that McPhail and his wife lodged with him and his wife. He had on one occasion visited Ann Walne's beerhouse in company with McPhail, travelling in McPhail's pony and cart.

John Walmsley, a cab-driver of Blackburn, said that on the evening of Tuesday 11 November – the day on which the murder was discovered – he had driven McPhail and George Woods in his cab on a 'pub-crawl' in Blackburn.

John Thirkell, a Grimsargh boy, reported finding a piece of flannel near the railway bridge close to his home. He later handed it to the police.

Sergeant Sleigh and Constable Howard of Blackburn said they had arrested McPhail, Carr and George Woods on Monday 1 December on instructions from McNab.

Superintendents Green and McNab then outlined their investigation of the crime, culminating in the arrest and charging of McPhail, George Woods and others. At one stage, McNab produced a statement which he said he had taken from Duncan McPhail at Kirkdale Gaol, Liverpool, before the committal proceedings. He proposed to read the statement to the court, but His Lordship said he would not allow this. 'The law is very jealous of statements made by prisoners to police officers,' he said.

The significance of this will be made clear in due course.

Cross-examined by Mr Pope on behalf of Woods, McNab agreed that the tell-tale footprints in the barn had not been found till almost a month after the murder. In the interim there had been hail, snow, freezing and thawing.

But of course the really important witnesses were the informers – or 'approvers' as they were referred to constantly during the trial – Chorley Tom Bowling and Benjamin Hartley.

Hartley repeated his original statement and held to it in the face of strong cross-examination. He freely admitted his own part in the affair. Snow was falling, he agreed, on the night in question. He was not the last man in Ann Walne's bedroom –

George Woods was. He denied he had 'gone back and finished her'. He was in work as a power-loom weaver, he said, and that was the first time he had ever gone out on a robbery.

Bowling agreed he was known as 'Chorley Tom'. He was on intimate terms with McPhail and knew Woods, Carr and Hartley. On 20 November – ten days after the murder – he had gone to McPhail's house, ostensibly to borrow his pony and cart, and had spoken to McPhail from the street when he came to a bedroom window. They had discussed the Ribchester murder. Chorley Tom had asked McPhail if he thought Davis – still in custody – was guilty of the crime. McPhail had replied, 'Is he hell!' He had then gone on to admit his own guilt and had named Carr, Hartley, William Woods and George Woods as his accomplices.

'He told me something of what had happened,' Chorley Tom said, continuing his evidence. 'I asked him, "Why did you have to kill her?" and he said, "She should have told us where the money was." I then asked him. "Will you give me something from the place?" McPhail replied, "We only got money." I then threatened to tell Mr Higgs [Police Superintendent at Blackburn] and later on I did so. I am a gamekeeper,' he finished. 'I don't agree with murder.'

Cross-examined, Chorley Tom said, 'I left McPhail with those words on my lips. I got locked up myself through this.'

He agreed he had once been on a poaching trip with these men when they had broken into a house, but denied having taken any part in the burglary. They had also told him about breaking into another house. He admitted that when he went to McPhail's house on that occasion he had known about the £100 reward offered for information.

Mr Higgin QC made a short closing speech for the Crown, no more than a summary of the evidence, which he said was clear proof of the guilt of both accused.

No witnesses were called for the defence. In his closing address on behalf of McPhail, Mr Jones said, among other things:

> We are asked to believe by the prosecution that McPhail confessed to this murder to a notorious bad character like Chorley Tom. McPhail is in a good way of business as a hawker, so it is unlikely he would stoop to such a deed for

the price of a cow. Would he ruin himself for four pounds ten shillings and sixpence? In fact he made no response at all to Chorley Tom's threats to expose him to the police: gave him no money: did not panic or attempt to cover up. Bowling cannot corroborate the approver, Hartley, for Bowling is an approver too – and even a hundred approvers cannot corroborate each other. On his own admission, Hartley was present at the crime – but was McPhail? There is no identification of McPhail as one of the four. No footprints were found of McPhail. There is not a scintilla of evidence against him.

Hartley, the approver, was the most guilty. He held the old woman's head while blows were struck. Now he incriminates others to save himself. There were no marks on McPhail: not a scratch.

Mr Jones alluded at some length to the bad character of Chorley Tom Bowling, making a strong point of the manner in which Bowling had asked for a share of the plunder.

In conclusion, he said, 'I trust the jury will remove all prejudice from their minds and administer true justice to McPhail – and through that, justice to society at large.'

In speaking on behalf of Woods, Mr Pope also attacked the 'approvers', Chorley Tom and Hartley. He produced an Army record which he said was that of George Woods, and tried to introduce it as evidence of his client's character, but the judge would not allow him to do so. Pope then went on:

Woods is not a bad character. He has no previous convictions. Generally, a man does not inaugurate his criminal career with a murder. As you have heard, the footprints in the barn were not found till nearly a month after the murder. The weather had been bad. They might easily have become distorted. After all, the footprint evidence was wrong in relation to the innocent man, Thomas Davis.

The murder was not premeditated [Pope said in conclusion]. The object was robbery. Do not in these times regard it as indispensable that because a murder has been committed, somebody must die for it.

The judge, Mr Baron Martin, appears to have summed up against McPhail and Woods.

'An approver is a competent witness,' he told the jury, 'and it is competent for the jury to convict on the evidence of an approver. For a number of years judges have been in the habit of advising juries *not* to convict on the unsupported evidence of an accomplice. But was this evidence not supported? Do you believe Hartley's evidence? Do you find it has been materially confirmed? If so, you are entitled to act on it.'

The jury retired and were out for some time. When they returned, they announced a verdict of 'Guilty' against both men but added a strong recommendation for mercy.

The judge clearly approved the verdict but, before passing sentence, spoke in somewhat scathing terms about the added recommendation. It would be recorded and passed to the proper authority, he said, but he could hold out no hope that it would be acted upon. He was totally unable to imagine why the jurors should wish such ruffians to be spared. Both must die the death of murderers. He then donned the black cap, pronounced sentence of death and ordered that the prisoners be removed from court.

As the final scene in the trial, the 'approver' Benjamin Hartley was arraigned on the murder charge. No evidence was offered against him, and he was formally acquitted.

Hartley's ordeal was not yet over, however. According to newspaper accounts of the time, large crowds waited at Blackburn and Cherry Tree railway stations in anticipation of his return. They were very angry and seemed intent on 'lynching' him. Attempts were made to smuggle him into the town by a later train, but many angry people were still present, and the police had to provide protection for the journey to his home in Pearson Street. That was accomplished, but the house was then beset by an angry mob, shouting, 'Turn out the murderer.' These words were chalked on the wall of the house, together with many others, including 'Hartley the murderer's house' and 'Hartley, the murderer of Ann Walne'.

The police managed to sneak him into the house of a neighbour, and only just in time. The mob then broke into Hartley's house and went on the rampage when they found themselves cheated. Hartley and his wife were then smuggled into a cab and taken to the house of a relation in Trinity Street. They left that house shortly afterwards and were last seen heading out of Blackburn on the Accrington road. The suggestion has since been made that with police assistance they fled the country.

A memorial (petition) numerously signed by citizens of Blackburn was forwarded by solicitors to the Home Secretary on behalf of George Woods, praying that Her Majesty Queen Victoria be advised to exercise her Royal Clemency. The petition was unsuccessful, there being no grounds, in the Home Secretary's view, for interfering with the due process of law.

A similar memorial for Duncan McPhail was 'hawked around the town' but obtained few signatories. In the event it was likewise rejected, but it is interesting to note that McPhail's memorial included a statement of confession from him.

This was the statement produced in court by Superintendent McNab and which the judge had prevented him from reading. After sentence had been passed, C.M. Collett, solicitor, of 29 Richmond Terrace, Blackburn, took the statement back to McPhail at Kirkdale Gaol and, after minor amendments, induced him to sign it. The statement read as follows:

I have known Chorley Tom for upwards of twelve months. It was Chorley Tom who planned the Ribchester Job and urged the others on. Dan Carr objected to Chorley Tom actually going on the job because he was not to be trusted. Chorley Tom has planned and been on other burglaries in the Ribchester area. He was in on the robbery of Mr Woodacre, the 'old miser'. He told me about the 'old miser' case a week earlier, when he tried to borrow my conveyance to go to Ribchester. He partially explained the purpose, which was to rob the old woman. I told him, 'No. My strawberry horse is too well known.'

I had met Ben Hartley at Preston Guild, three months before, when he was introduced to me by Chorley Tom. Eventually, the others inveigled me into going on the Walne job. We went on foot, because I wouldn't use my conveyance. On the way to her house I told the others, 'Now mind, whatever you do, don't hurt the old woman.'

McPhail's statement goes on to describe the enterprise much as Hartley had previously described it, with the difference that McPhail claimed a much more minor role.

'I said I would stay outside. Carr said, "OK. You keep watch," and he handed me a pistol. Carr lit the lamp and the others went in. I stood outside the window. I could see and hear the others rummaging about inside the house and when I heard the old woman screaming I had to go in and protest about what they were doing. Carr ordered me out, but I stayed in the house near to the window.'

Remarkably, McPhail goes on to describe the events upstairs: the blows, the searching of the bed, the tying of the woman's hands to the bed-rail with handkerchieves – and he adds: 'When George again asked her for the money, the old woman threw a small packet to the foot of the bed, and George picked it up. I supposed it contained money.'

All this he presents as hearsay, denying his own presence. Afterwards, on the way to Preston, a route he suggested because it was safer than going back to Blackburn, he received his share of the spoils from Woods.

'During the following days,' the statement continues, 'Chorley Tom went round each of us in turn, demanding money in return for his silence and saying, "There is a hundred pounds reward." Because we would not pay him, he went to the police.'

For me, the most interesting aspect of McPhail's statement is the fact that it was available *before* the trial, and the defence barristers knew very well it was. They must have been pleased when the judge refused to have it read to the jury – though in the long run the advantage was of no avail. Nor did it help much in the later application for clemency. But in view of what McPhail had to say about Chorley Tom, it becomes plain why Chorley Tom was cross-examined about his connection with previous burglaries.

On Saturday 25 April 1863 McPhail wrote a letter to his solicitor, Collett, which began: 'I embrace this, my last opportunity ...'

The letter arrived on Monday morning, and if it contained anything of significance, it was a day too late.

On Sunday 26 April Woods and McPhail were hanged in front of Kirkdale Gaol by the hangman Calcraft.

They had made no confession to the chaplain.

'Crowds collected before the gallows,' said a report in the *Guardian* newspaper of that date. 'The old passion for hanging is still in the land.'

13   The Cripple-Dwarf Case,
Nelson 1936

'Free' newspapers are by no means a phenomenon of the present day. At least one such organ existed in the year 1936. *The Gazette* was a regular publication and was distributed without charge to all houses and business premises in Nelson, Lancashire – which called for a considerable number of copies, even in those days. Its editor – and presumably also its proprietor – was Alderman E. Smith, leader of Nelson Socialists, though whether he used the newspaper as a vehicle for his political views is a matter for conjecture.

The issue of *The Gazette* for Tuesday 7 July 1936 carried in its 'Notes and Notions' column (which might or might not have been written by Alderman Smith) an item castigating the local police for their tardiness in proceeding with a case of murder.

'The man has been held in custody for some time,' the item complained. 'He has been remanded three times since arrested, and still no real evidence has been offered against him. It is time something was done about it. The police should expedite matters. Already the delay has led to rumours in the town. It is being suggested that *two other guilty men are walking free.*'

The man referred to was Max Mayer Haslam, a bow-legged dwarf. He had been arrested about 8.30 p.m. on Monday 22 June, initially on a charge of stealing jewellery. On the following day he was further charged with the wilful murder of Ruth Clarkson, aged seventy-four, a recluse who lived alone at 56 Clayton Street, Nelson.

As to the 'two other guilty men' rumoured to be walking free, it is anyone's guess as to whom *The Gazette* had in mind – and yet, when the full facts of the case are examined, certain hints are revealed that might point to possible suspects.

Max Mayer Haslam was twenty-three years of age, born at Heywood, Lancashire, on 12 June 1913. He had three older brothers and two younger sisters.

From birth he suffered from a disease of the bones so crippling that he could not walk at all until he was nine years old. As a result he suffered from bowed legs and stunted growth, so that at the age of twenty-three he stood only four feet seven inches tall. He was ultra-conscious of his own deformity, and that no doubt explains why he was always backward at school. He was a 'loner', morose and ill-tempered and an abnormally deep thinker. He did not get on well with other children. He lived with his parents at 40 Miller Street, Heywood, but until the age of sixteen he was under the care of Heywood Crippled Children's Committee.

At some stage during his childhood, members of that committee approached the boy's father, George Edward Haslam, with a suggestion that his son should receive corrective treatment for his bowed legs. However, Haslam senior refused his consent and so nothing could be done. It is tempting to wonder if the boy ever knew of the suggestion, and if so, what effect his father's refusal of consent had on him, but those are questions without answers.

Haslam left school on 15 July 1927, at the age of fourteen, and found work as a 'reacher-over' at Burns' Spinning Mill, Oldham. According to his father, he threw off his depression on starting work and seemed to forget about his deformity. Sadly, in March 1934 Burns' Mill closed down, owing to loss of trade, and he became unemployed. Not surprisingly, his brooding and irritability once more gripped him. As a reacher-over he had been earning 19 shillings a week, a quite respectable wage. Out of work and on the dole he received only 12s.6d. – but, more to the point, he had time on his hands.

It seems certain that Haslam's rapid fall from grace began at that time. For seven years he had gone regularly to work and, as far as the records show, had behaved himself very well. In just two more years his conduct took him to damnation. But in case too much sympathy should be felt for Haslam, it is as well to bear in mind that effectively he was his own executioner. Once he had chosen that mode of life, he became a cocky, persistent and very determined criminal.

Out of work and with reduced income, he began stealing and was quickly caught. At Heywood Police Court, on 21 April 1934, only weeks after the mill closed, he was convicted of club-breaking and had three cases of larceny taken into consideration. He was sentenced to six months imprisonment *without* hard labour.

When he was released from prison, there was still no work, and he had not learned the lessons of imprisonment any better than those at school. He continued to commit crimes. On 19 July 1935, on charges of burglary and office-breaking with four similar offences taken into consideration, the judge at Preston Quarter Sessions sentenced him to twelve months hard labour.

He was released from Strangeways Prison on 9 May 1936, and eight months later he was back in the same prison, this time to await hanging for murder.

The path Haslam followed to the gallows began at the prison gates following his release on 9 May. His first journey was to his father's home at Heywood, where he told the story that he was '... working on an estate, cleaning motor cars and doing a bit of gardening'. There was no truth in it, but it gave him an excuse for not staying at home. He gave his father a little money and then left.

Two days later, at 10.20 a.m. on Tuesday 12 May, he booked in at Primrose Bank Institution, Burnley, known locally as 'the workhouse', and was supplied with a bed. He stayed there for more than two weeks, being booked out on the morning of Saturday 30 May. During his stay he struck up an acquaintance with another 'workhouse' inmate, fifty-six-year-old Thomas Hogan.

At a later time, Hogan was to relate a conversation which he had had rather one-sidedly with Haslam. Here is the gist of it.

'Do you know Nelson? I am going to see an old lady, a relation of mine who lives in Clayton Street, and if she doesn't give me some money to go on the road with, I'll do something to her that I may be sorry for. The old woman is of independent means. She's a miser, and it's about time she gave me something. All she can think about is that bit of a dog.'

If Hogan spoke the truth, his account was strong evidence of premeditation on Haslam's part, for it clearly forecast the events that were to follow. It also implied prior knowledge of the victim, which later evidence suggests he did not have, and a relationship between Haslam and the victim which, as far as I have been able to discover, did not exist. Hogan did not report the conversation to the police until much later, when he knew that there had been a murder and that Haslam was at least suspected of it, and no doubt he also knew details of the story, since they were being freely bandied abroad. Frankly, I think Hogan used what he had learned to invent the story, as a means of drawing attention to himself in a well-known form of glory-grabbing.

And yet, as will be seen, Haslam was a great talker, and the phraseology does sound very like his. So perhaps I am misjudging Hogan. Perhaps Haslam did have prior knowledge.

It is well established that Haslam did go to Nelson. He appeared in the town centre on 30 May, the same day on which he had left the Burnley 'workhouse', and was seen there by James William Davieson, aged twenty-seven, an unemployed labourer. He and Davieson spoke together. Haslam said he was looking for somewhere to live, and Davieson suggested he should share his room at the lodging-house at 69 Vernon Street, Nelson. Davieson himself had moved in only that day, but there was a spare bed in the room and the landlord would let Haslam have it. They went there together, and terms were agreed.

Also living at 69 Vernon Street, in a different room, was Thomas Barlow, aged twenty-two, an unemployed labourer.

This meeting and the lodging arrangements were described by Davieson when he was later interviewed by the police, and something about the account has a hollow ring. It seems a remarkable coincidence that Davieson should find lodgings in the town, then on the very same day go to the town centre, speak to a total stranger and invite him to share those lodgings. When one considers that Haslam was a loner, morose, unable to mix well, his rapid striking-up of a friendship with Davieson, the very man who had lodgings to offer, seems even more odd. Had they met before? Had they come to Nelson together? Was the whole thing pre-arranged – a criminal venture in the making? And what about Thomas Barlow, for he had a major role in what was to follow? Was he the new acquaintance he was supposed to be?

If these questions ever arose at the time, no effort seems to have been made to find answers – and more than fifty years on, I have tried and failed.

What is recorded is that Haslam, Davieson and the third man, Thomas Barlow, began to spend their time together right from the first day of meeting. Haslam had ceased to be a loner and was hardly ever seen without Davieson, Barlow or both. If the other two are to be believed, Haslam did most of the talking, and what they talked about was crime.

According to Davieson, he and Haslam were together in the town centre, only a few days after Haslam's arrival in Nelson, when Haslam said, 'I'm going to knock the chap out at the coal shop in the arcade.' He made no move then towards carrying out the threat, but a day or so afterwards, when the two were together again, he picked up a piece of rusty iron bar he found lying in the street and said, 'I'll go and do that Jew-boy in at the gold shop. But he has an assistant, so I'll go to the arcade and do the coal chap.'

Davieson went with him to the arcade but would not enter. He waited outside, in the street. Haslam went into the arcade with the iron bar under his coat but came out a few minutes later.

'There's a lousy cop just come out of yonder,' he said. 'It must be well watched.'

Much more to the point of this story, about a week after that Davieson and Barlow were together in the town when Haslam joined them. Passing at that moment was an old woman, leading a fox-terrier dog, and Barlow said she was called Ruth Clarkson. The following conversation then took place.

Davieson:	'Look at that dirty old bugger.'
Barlow:	'She has more bloody money than us.'
Haslam:	'How do you know that?'
Barlow:	'Well, I used to live back door to her.'
Davieson:	'She doesn't look so prosperous.'
Haslam:	'Where is she going now?'
Barlow:	'Looks like she's going shopping. She's got a carrier bag.'

On the evening of Monday 15 June the three men were together again in Scotland Road, Nelson, when Haslam said: 'I want to buy a tyre-lever.' He went into Hebden's shop, 71

Scotland Road and came out carrying a package. He handed it to the others in turn, saying: 'Feel the weight of that.'

'How much did it cost?' Davieson wondered.

'One and six,' Haslam told him.

He unwrapped the parcel and showed them a tyre-lever. They inspected it in turn, and he then wrapped it up again. Afterwards, all three men went to the pictures.

That night, when Davieson and Haslam were in their room, Davieson asked him, 'Where have you put the tyre-lever?'

'Mind your own business,' Haslam said, 'or I'll let you feel the weight of it.'

Their next meeting in the town centre, about 2 p.m. on Friday 19 June, was brief. After they had exchanged a few words, Haslam said to the others: 'I think I'll take a look at the market.'

He walked away from them as though heading for the market, but they were suspicious, so they followed him at a distance. He took a roundabout route through the town and eventually came to Clayton Street. They watched him go to the front door of number 56, where he knocked twice but received no response. He then went round towards the back of the house, and they could not follow without being seen. They walked back to the town centre and waited. After some time, Haslam rejoined them as though coming from the direction of the market, and when he said, 'There is nothing on the market', *they knew he was lying.* They wondered what Haslam was up to, but neither man saw fit to challenge him. As they were strolling through the town, Haslam said: 'The landlady will be jumping on me. I don't know how I am going to pay her this week. She won't let me keep strapping up' (living on credit).

After some discussion about what to do, they decided to spend an hour in nearby Walverden Park and set off together in that direction. But once more Haslam left the others, saying: 'I'll join you in about five minutes.'

He did not join them. The next time Davieson saw Haslam was about 8.15 a.m. on the following day, when he came into the Vernon Street lodgings having been out all night. He was then wearing a brown suit and a brown trilby hat (his own), and his face and hands were dirty. He said to Davieson and Barlow: 'I have some jewellery. Where can I sell it?'

Barlow told him there were several jewellers' shops in Nelson and others in Colne and Burnley. Haslam then said: 'I have killed a dog to get it. The house was dirty. I spilled some paint, and it just missed me. I strung the dog up and pinched it with a screwdriver to see if it was dead.'

All the above conversations were recounted by Thomas William Davieson in a statement he made later to the police. There was a lot more, but it can conveniently be left for the moment.

Thomas Barlow also made a lengthy statement along much the same lines. It differed from Davieson's account, but not so markedly as to fall short of corroboration. For example, in repeating what Haslam had said about the dog, Barlow's version was: 'It was like a rag shop where I have been. I tied some string round the dog's neck. I hit it with my fist as it was coming at me and then strung it up.'

And it was Barlow, according to his statement, who had first pointed out the Clayton Street house to Haslam.

'Yes,' he said in response to a query from Haslam. 'She lives right opposite that traffic pole at the bottom of New Brown Street.'

The first intimation the police had that something was amiss came when a man named Bracewell Morville, an unemployed grocer (?) of 54 Thomas Street, Nelson, went to Nelson police station about 3 p.m. on Monday 22 June. Little is recorded about Morville, but reading between the lines he was a public-spirited citizen or a 'copper's nark', depending on one's point of view. He spoke to Detective Constables Peter Gregson and Isaac Fell.

'The little chap,' he said, 'has killed a dog at 52, 54 or 56 Clayton Street, and he has got some jewellery. Go and tell Mr [Detective Chief Inspector] Fenton if he goes to Gibson's he'll see whether he has sold a watch or not, and if he goes to Jolly's, the little chap has had some chains valued there.'

Bracewell Morville told the officers he knew about these things because 'Davieson told me.'

Chief Inspector Fenton and his men visited the shops of Allan Dodd Gibson, 22 Scotland Road, and Walter Holt (Jolly's) at 55 Netherfield Road. As a result of what they learned there they went on to visit every jewellery shop in the area, some on that day, others on succeeding days.

Someone had indeed been hawking jewellery from shop to

shop, and from descriptions supplied by jewellers it was evidently 'the little chap' Haslam. He had managed to sell some items, and the police soon recovered a ladies' gold breast watch, a silver brooch, a silver mesh purse, a gold ring and a gold neck-chain and pendant.

Hot on the trail of something, Detective Constables Gregson and Fell made enquiries in Clayton Street. By eliminating other addresses they learned that the only place where a theft might have occurred was number 56. The lady living there, Ruth Clarkson, was something of a recluse. She had not been seen since 7.30 p.m. on the previous Friday, when a friend, Gerty Bowes, of 49 George Street, Nelson, had seen her walking with her dog. When the detectives called at 56 Clayton Street, they found the doors locked, and there was no answer to their knocking. But the visit was not entirely wasted. On the back door they found fresh gouge marks, suggesting an attempt to break open the door.

On the advice of neighbours the officers went to 37 Kendal Street, Nelson, home of Sisson Dobney and his second wife, Ivy. They were friends of Miss Clarkson. Sisson Dobney told them he had known the woman for thirty years, mainly because she had been on close terms with his first wife, who was now dead. Shown the items of jewellery, he identified the silver mesh purse as one he had bought for his first wife; later, with his approval, she had given it to Ruth Clarkson. The new Mrs Dobney had known the old lady for only about three years but had been friendly with her in that time. She had never been inside Miss Clarkson's house but had communicated with her regularly by letter or by slipping notes through her door. She had a small white dog called 'Roy' which was a good tenter (barker) but would not bite. Miss Clarkson, she said, was very careful. She would not open her door to anyone, even relations. She was very religious too. She had been expected at a meeting of the Bethel Evangelical Church, held in rooms over Brennands' Café in the town on 17 June, but she had not turned up.

At 8 p.m. on the same date – Monday 22 June – Detective Chief Inspector Fenton, accompanied by Detective Constables Fell, Gregson and James Rothwell, went to 56 Clayton Street and gained entry by forcing the front door. They were amazed and no doubt disgusted by what they found.

The house was indescribably filthy. Mountains of litter covered almost every part of the downstairs rooms. Torn newspapers, old clothing and rags were piled everywhere to a height of three feet, and on top of the piles were scattered boxes, cartons, tins and broken furniture. The table was piled with dirty crockery, milk bottles, empty jamjars and the remains of food.

Ruth Clarkson was lying dead among piles of rubbish in the kitchen, and the only way they could move about was by stepping over her body. She was clothed in filthy rags tied together with string. The lower part of her body was naked. There were very obvious wounds to her head, which was covered in blood, and more gouts of blood were splashed on furniture, the piles of litter and various parts of the wall, including a picture hanging there. Drawers and cupboards had been ransacked and the contents strewn about. A tyre-lever, a piece of iron railing and a block of wood, all heavily bloodstained, were lying close to the body.

On going upstairs, the officers found more accumulated rubbish and disarray, but the most impressive sight was the body of a white fox-terrier in the main bedroom. It was hanging from the bed-rail by a piece of string tied round its neck, and already there were maggots crawling in the flesh.

The back door, on which gouge marks had been seen earlier, was locked with a box-type lock, and the key was missing. But it was obvious that the door had been opened by force, for an inner bolt had been broken off and was lying on the floor at the foot of the door. The police were convinced the killer had entered that way and re-locked the door with the key after leaving.

Other police officers were brought to the house and left on guard, and the police surgeon was sent for. The four detectives then left the house in search of Max Mayer Haslam – and within a matter of minutes they chanced upon him in Pendle Street, Nelson. Chief Inspector Fenton cautioned him and told him he was being arrested on a charge of stealing jewellery from 56 Clayton Street, which was a useful 'holding' charge. The murder was not mentioned at that time.

Haslam said: 'I admit selling that jewellery but it is my own. I have had it a good many years.'

At the time of Haslam's arrest, Thomas Barlow was with him, and both men were taken to Nelson police station. When he was searched, the following items were found on Haslam: a pair of kid gloves, a pair of spectacles, a silver signet ring, a long rolled-gold chain, a gold-coloured brooch and a key for a box-type lock. He was also wearing a metal wristlet watch.

Asked about this property, he said: 'It is my own. I have had it for a long time. I told the man at the shop it was my father's but that isn't true. I bought it off different people but I don't know who from. The key belongs to the back door of my father's house.'

The police were suspicious of the whole explanation and soon proved the last part of it to be false. The key was taken to Heywood and tried in all the locks at 40 Miller Street. It fitted none of them. But when it was tried in the back door at 56 Clayton Street, it easily operated the lock.

In the course of police enquiries that followed, a variety of witnesses had their tales to tell. Some have already been dealt with, and what follows is a selection from the others.

William Joseph Audley, manager of a pawnbroker's shop at 24 Leeds Road, Nelson, told of a man of Haslam's description pawning a pair of shoes on Saturday 20 June and redeeming them two days later.

Edith Edmondson, aged thirty-nine, of 249 Railway Street, Nelson, said she knew Ruth Clarkson very well. The old lady owned a lot of old-fashioned jewellery. Edmondson was not able positively to identify the items the police showed her. However, she did attend the Nelson mortuary, where she identified the body of Ruth Clarkson.

Mona Eleanor Hart, of 48 Clayton Street, identified Haslam as a man she had seen knocking on Ruth Clarkson's door about 3.30 p.m. on Friday 19 June.

John Harold Hebden said he kept an ironmongers' shop at 71 Scotland Road, Nelson. A few days before the murder he had sold a tyre-lever to a man who looked like Haslam. Shown a tyre-lever by the police, he said it was 'similar, but rubbed at the end'.

Thomas Routledge, who with his wife ran a lodging-house at 69 Vernon Street, Nelson, remembered the occasion when Haslam stayed out all night. He had seen Haslam come in and join Barlow and Davieson and had heard him say: 'I have killed a dog and strung it up. The house where I have been to was filthy. Jamjars all over the table. They looked as though they had been there for a twelvemonth.'

Believing that Haslam must be joking, Routledge had done nothing about it. He was the more surprised when Haslam came to him not long afterwards and paid him his back rent of 25 shillings. He actually received a shilling more, and when he offered change, Haslam told him, 'Get yourself some cigs with it.'

Dorothy Riley of Burnley said she was a niece of Mary Jane Riley who had lived as Miss Clarkson's companion until her death about eight years previously. Her aunt had owned a lot of jewellery. In particular she remembered a long gold chain which her aunt had worn round her neck with the ends tucked into her skirt. She could identify the chain positively and thought she recognized most of the other items.

William Edward Riley of 243 Manchester Road, Nelson, a nephew of the same Mary Jane Riley, said he did not know about jewellery but knew his aunt had left all her personal effects to Ruth Clarkson. His wife, Ada Riley, did know about the jewellery. She thought the items the police showed her were 'similar'.

William Ernest Halliwell, jeweller, of 59 Market Street, Colne, identified the ladies' gold breast watch as one he had sold some years ago to another customer. However, he was also able to state that to his knowledge the watch had passed through several hands until it became the property of Ruth Clarkson.

There were other witnesses – and of course there were the statements of James William Davieson and Thomas Barlow, which can now continue, dealing first with Davieson's statement.

After Haslam had told them about killing the dog, all three men went to Walverden Park, where Haslam showed them a number of items of jewellery, including the ones later recovered by the police. He told them: 'I got these from the house down yonder in Clayton Street. What will they be worth?'

Davieson told him: 'About eight quid. Try Jolly's down Leeds Road.'

Later that day they met in the town, and Davieson suggested they should go into the Nelson Hotel for a drink.

'No,' Haslam said. 'The jacks might see me flashing money about.'

They went instead to the Bull Hotel, where Haslam showed them a large silver-coloured watch in a leather wrist case.

'What's this worth?' he said.

'Silver isn't worth much,' Davieson told him.

Haslam said: 'I'd better throw the case away before Fenton comes smelling round.'

They went to the Majestic Cinema together and after seeing the film walked down Scotland Road. Haslam took the case off the watch and dropped the case down a street grating.

In their shared bedroom, about midnight, Haslam asked him: 'Do you know where I could get shut of a corpse? Could I get shut up Coldwell, where that horse were drowned in that bog and never came up?'

'What do you mean?' Davieson asked him.

'I was just kidding,' Haslam replied. Even so, within minutes he returned to the theme, saying: 'If you threw owt in that there place, would it come up?'

'I wouldn't like to be bloody well thrown in,' Davieson said.

In the middle of that night Davieson was wakened by strange sounds, to find Haslam washing his socks in the sink. He asked him why he was doing that, and Haslam said: 'To get the blood off.'

Davieson: 'You haven't done the old woman in where you said you'd been?'

Haslam: 'No. I only just walloped her. I bet she thought McAvoy [a well-known boxer] had hit her.'

Later, about 6 a.m., Davieson saw Haslam putting the still wet socks on and advised him against it.

'You are fearful bothered about my socks,' Haslam said. 'If I hear much more off you, I'll tap you, like I tapped her.'

Thomas Barlow, after agreeing with the parts of Davieson's statement that included him, had this to say: 'Haslam paid for all the beer in the Bull Hotel and also for seats for me and Davieson at the Majestic Cinema. Later on, when Davieson was not there, he said to me, "Where can we go where it's quiet?" I said, "How quiet?" He said, "Very quiet. I don't want anyone else to hear." '

They began to walk along Pendle Street, and Haslam said, 'I have property. You like money, don't you? Can you drive a car?'

Barlow answered that he did, and he could, and he asked, 'What do you want?'

Haslam said: 'Take a body up Coldwell and dump it in a swamp.'

Barlow asked him what he was talking about, and Haslam said: 'I've done a woman in.'

Barlow said he was not prepared to help in that way because it was too dangerous, but Haslam said: 'There's £200 in it for you.'

'I'll consider that,' Barlow responded.

But he did not have time to consider it, for at that moment the detectives appeared and spoke to them. They were both taken to the police station. Haslam was charged with stealing jewellery, and Barlow began to make the long statement, the gist of which has been given above.

There was plenty of evidence from the scene of the crime.

The police surgeon, Dr Ritchie, pronounced life extinct, though he made only a superficial examination of the body. He described the house as a shambles. There was an upturned chair near the body. In addition to the head wounds there was blood on the legs of the deceased. He also examined Haslam and found a number of small scars behind his left ear and on his chest, apparently made by fingernails. The scars were two to three days old.

Detective Sergeant William Henry Mercer came from Rochdale on 23 June to examine the house. He collected a variety of exhibits, including the tyre-lever, iron bar and block of wood, also a screwdriver, an assortment of hairs from the dead dog, and several chunks of wallpaper and plaster from the walls which were marked with bloodstains and grooved depressions. He was present when Detective Constable Gregson operated the back-door lock with the key found in Haslam's possession.

Gregson took further samples of dog hairs from bedside rugs in the room in Vernon Street occupied by Haslam and Davieson, and also hair samples from a live dog that lived at the house.

Detective Inspector James Duncan, Headquarters Fingerprint Department, found a palmar impression on the upturned chair and later gave evidence that it was identical with a palm print taken from Haslam's right hand. The chair had bloodstains on it.

At the request of the Chief Constable, Captain A.F. Hordern, the scene was visited by Arnold Renshaw MD, BS (Lond.), DPH (Manch.-Cantab.), Director of the Laboratory of Applied Pathology and Preventive Medicine, Manchester. The body had not been removed when he arrived. He saw three severe head wounds at once, and others were found later, at the mortuary, when the blood had been washed away.

Renshaw described the clothing on the body (listed later, at the time of stripping) as an old grey knitted woollen shawl, a tattered and patched coat of macintosh material, another tattered coat, a frock tied together with string, a wool and cotton chemise very torn and soaked with blood, a vest, black corsets and a red flannel bodybelt. The house was dirty and verminous, and the bed also verminous. Of the weapons at the scene, the iron tyre-lever appeared to be the one that had made the wounds. It had been rubbed bright at one end in an effort to sharpen it.

Great violence had obviously been used on Ruth Clarkson. Her body was covered with bruises and injuries.

After the body had been removed to the mortuary, the pathologist carried out a post-mortem examination. The skull was fractured in various places, the jaw fractured and the fingers of both hands also fractured. The cause of death was, he said, shock and haemorrhage following multiple injuries.

He also conducted a post-mortem examination on the fox-terrier dog. The cord was tied tightly round its neck. There was a bruise on its chest consistent with a kick, but death was due to hanging. The carcase was maggot-infested. It had been dead for at least three days and possibly longer.

Renshaw then examined the prisoner and amongst other things took samples of hair from his head. He described Haslam as 'a young, short adult suffering from the obvious deformity of bowing and lack of growth of legs'. He found a scratch, or possibly a dog bite, on the back of Haslam's right index finger. There were bloodstains and creosote and paint stains on most of his clothing but not on his shirt or socks.

All the items of clothing Haslam was wearing when arrested (brown suit, trilby hat, brown shoes, socks, shirt and tie), plus other clothing found at his lodgings, were sent to Dr Renshaw's laboratory in Manchester for further pathological examination. The samples taken from the scene and from Haslam's room were also sent.

Renshaw later submitted a very long, detailed and comprehensive report on all the items he had examined, but only a summary of his findings is necessary here.

As well as blood and paint on clothing he had found traces of human blood on the toecap of a left boot belonging to Haslam. There were striking similarities between hairs found on the clothing and samples taken from other places. He had made many comparison slides, and four comparisons in particular had produced positive results. These were: hairs from the boot corresponded with hairs from the dead dog; hairs from Haslam's jacket likewise matched those of the dead dog; hairs found on his waistcoat were from the living dog at his lodgings, and hairs found on the rusty iron bar were from the dead dog.

Dr Renshaw later displayed all his slides in court.

When Haslam was charged with the murder, he replied, 'Not guilty. That's all I have to say.'

An inquest into the death of Ruth Clarkson was opened and adjourned in view of pending criminal proceedings.

As mentioned at the outset, Max Mayer Haslam appeared several times for remand at the magistrates' court, much to the chagrin of Alderman Smith and *The Gazette*, and it must have been a great relief to the public of Nelson when he was eventually brought there again and committal proceedings took place.

Haslam persisted in his 'Not guilty' plea, his defence being a simple denial of the crime. But the legion of witnesses called to testify against him made his cause a lost one – and none gave more telling evidence than James William Davieson and Thomas Barlow. The issue can never have been in doubt if the magistrates believed what those two gentleman had to say – and since they were never charged as accomplices or accessories, nor was such a suggestion ever made, there was no question of their testimonies being tainted so as to call for corroboration. Even if it had been, there was corroboration enough from other witnesses.

At the close of those proceedings Haslam was committed in custody to stand trial at the next assizes for the county.

When the trial opened at Manchester Assizes in December, the pattern of the hearing was little different from what had gone before. Medical evidence was called to show that there was no history of insanity in Haslam or his blood relations. Apart from cross-examining the witnesses, the defence had hardly anything to offer in rebuttal of the prosecution case. Eventually, on 10 December 1936, Haslam was convicted and sentenced to death.

He appealed, but the sentence was confirmed, and when his solicitors launched a petition for clemency, there was very little public support. The Home Secretary found no grounds for interfering with the due process of law.

At the same assizes, sentence of death was also passed on George Royle, convicted of killing Mrs Mary Josephine Holden in a case widely publicized as 'The East Lancs Road Murder'. The Home Secretary must have been more impressed by the petition submitted for Royle. It was approved, and Royle's sentence was commuted to one of life imprisonment.

Haslam was hanged at Strangeways Prison on 4 February 1937. He had made known his intention of refusing to see any of his family prior to the hanging and remained steadfast in that resolve. His father complained to no avail that he had not seen him for four months. His brother and sister-in-law went to the prison but were not admitted.

The days of public hanging were long gone, of course, and only the usual officials had the doubtful privilege of witnessing the execution. It must surely have been a more than usually distasteful spectacle. Though not particularly squeamish, I can never think of Max Mayer Haslam without visualizing his squat body, with its short bow-legs, dangling on the end of a rope.

There was much public disturbance in the street outside the prison. Barriers were erected and no person was allowed within fifty yards of the prison gates. Spurred on by Mrs van der Elst, a wealthy opponent of capital punishment, the crowd joined in singing 'Abide with me', to the accompaniment of music which Mrs van der Elst broadcast by loudspeaker from her car.

'Another state murder has just been committed,' she announced over the same loudspeaker when the sentence was carried out. 'Another insane man has been sent into eternity.'

And at 9.15 a.m., as the macabre procedure of posting notices of death took place, she broadcast the music of 'Nearer my God to Thee' and the crowd joined in the singing.

I have no doubt Haslam paid a just penalty. The evidence against him – even without the statements of Davieson and Barlow – convinces me of his guilt.

But I have to admit to feeling some disquiet about the parts played by the other two men. Were they the two described by *The Gazette* as rumoured to be 'guilty, but walking free'? Who can say with any certainty?

However, the distinct impression comes through to me that they were rather more closely involved in Haslam's activities than they ever stated. The damning things they said about him were not volunteered but elicited during questioning by the police. Parts of their statements, at least by implication and some would say expressly, revealed their own criminal tendencies. But in respect of the murder they were careful to blame Haslam for everything and exonerate themselves.

I can't help wondering what might have happened if the police had not discovered the murder for a few more days. Would Haslam have managed to raise the offered £200? Would Barlow – and Davieson too, perhaps – have helped him to dispose of the body? That dreadful bog at Coldwell was said to be very deep. Things that went in there never came up.

There is one further matter worth mentioning.

On 25 June, at Nelson police station, an identification parade was held at which Haslam was exhibited to witnesses. Somehow the police managed to find nine other men ranging in height from four feet six inches to five feet four inches, and they lined them up with Haslam.

I would not personally have thought such a parade was necessary, or even fair. His appearance, as described, was so unusual and distinctive that he must have stood out, even among other small people.

Nevertheless, I was surprised to learn that, of nine witnesses who saw that parade, only five positively identified Max Mayer Haslam.

14   A Tragi-Comedy of Errors, Tottington 1871

Human frailty lies at the root of all crime. It spurs the evildoer, unmans his victim, handicaps the administration of justice and sometimes misdirects the hands and hearts of those who would see justice done. As a conclusion to this anthology I have chosen an instance which illustrates human frailty in all these facets and which at its end leaves the observer with lingering doubts as to who was right and who wrong.

Tottington is a small village situated in a charming and virtually bypassed valley, midway between the towns of Bury and Ramsbottom in Lancashire. Its sparse economy grew from a handful of cotton mills, some still operating, others now lying in ruins. I know the village well. My family moved to Tottington in 1931, when I was three years old, and I lived happily there until I was twenty. There was no Brookside in my day. The small group of stone cottages adjoining Harwood Road was demolished around the turn of the century. But the remains were still to be seen: scraps of blue-plastered walls, stone sills and lintels, decayed window frames and solidly packed ashtips, the whole overgrown with willow herb and nettles and dandelions. The brook for which the cottages were named still ran limpid between blackened hillocks of petrified rubbish. For the knowing it was the source of sticklebacks, loaches and bullheads, to be trapped and carried home in water-filled jamjars.

In August 1871, among the several families living in Brookside were the Huttons, James and Elizabeth, and seven of their surviving children: Andrew, aged nineteen, Charles, fifteen,

William, eleven, Thomas, 'over ten', David, seven, Samuel, four, and one daughter, Alice Jane, aged seventeen. Their eldest son, John, aged twenty-one was married and living away.

James Hutton was a native of Scotland but had lived in Tottington for more than twenty years. He ran a small business as a bespoke tailor, working from his home. His wife, Elizabeth, was Tottington born, as were all the children.

At 9 a.m. on Wednesday 9 August 1871 James Hutton went to Tottington police station and informed Police Constable Reuben Barton that his youngest son, Samuel, had died suddenly, following a short illness. There would be several accounts of the events leading to the death – some of them at slight variance – but broadly speaking the facts were these.

About 4.30 p.m. on the previous day, the child had gone into the house next door, occupied by William and Elizabeth Scholes, who were close friends of the Huttons. At that time Mrs Scholes was present, and so was Elizabeth Hutton, Samuel's mother. She had gone there to bake a cake and was waiting for the oven to heat up before putting in the mixture.

In the words of Mrs Scholes, 'Sammy lay on the floor across the hearth. He slung his legs out as though they didn't belong to his body. I said, "If you go to sleep there, Sammy, I'll put you under the stairs where the dog lives." He seemed very tired. His mother told him, "You had better go home and lie on the sofa." He went out of the house, still slinging his legs as if they didn't belong to him.'

When Elizabeth Hutton went home, about 5 p.m., Samuel was lying on the sofa as he had been told. He appeared listless and didn't have much to say, and when she asked him if he felt ill, he answered with a nod. In the course of that evening he was seen by most of the family and by several neighbours. He asked his sister, Alice, for a 'butty', and she made him some bread and butter whilst somebody else boiled the kettle and brewed him a cup of tea. It is not certain whether he ate anything. Asked about it later, Alice thought he did not eat but drank half the tea. Others thought he had eaten a little. He was drowsy and slept for two hours, then, still complaining of illness, was undressed and taken to bed. His father said he had done that but he retracted it later, introducing another little doubt.

What is certain is that around 4.30 on the morning of 9 August the household was aroused by the child's moaning. His mother thought he was very ill. She and others made him some bread and butter and tea, but once again it is unclear whether he ate or drank. Mrs Scholes was sent for to assist. 'Give him some castor oil,' she advised and, because she sold castor oil as a sideline, she took Mrs Hutton next door, where, 'I weighed her an ounce.' Returning to the sickbed, Mrs Scholes gave Samuel a teaspoonful of castor oil. The child looked very poorly. 'He ground his teeth and shut his eyes. His breathing was short. It was hard work to breathe.'

James Hutton set off to fetch the doctor. He went first to the Tottington surgery, where Dr Robert Harris MRCS had a subsidiary practice, but there was no reply to his knocking. Dr Harris lived in Bury, where he had his main practice in combination with Drs Crompton and Ashworth. Hutton went back home alone, but his wife told him, 'You'd better go to Bury', so he set off again, to walk to Dr Harris's main surgery in Stanley Street, Bury.

The doctor was not so obliging as perhaps he might have been. 'Hutton got there between five and six in the morning,' he said later, 'and asked me to go with him to the house. I had been up all night with other patients and objected on that account, but I could have gone if he had pressed me. He asked me instead for "a little medicine" which he said he could get made up at Tottington. I took it he meant at my surgery in Tottington.'

The doctor visited the Huttons later in the day, but by then Samuel was dead. He had died about 6 a.m. in the presence of neighbours and members of the family.

For Dr Harris and PC Barton this was an unhappy but commonplace event. The policeman took details for his report. The doctor issued a certificate of death, an action he soon had cause to regret, and when he was taken mildly to task about it later, his explanation scarcely mended matters.

'I'm not sure if I gave it then, or the day after,' he said. 'It was not on a registrar's form: just two lines on a piece of paper. It certified death, not *cause* of death. I issued it because the father asked for it. He wanted it in order to collect some money from a burial club. When I gave the certificate I knew there would be an inquest. I had spoken to Constable Barton.'

Suspicion that Samuel might not have died naturally arose on

Thursday 10 August, the day after the death, when an inquest opened at 'the house of Betty Pilkington', the Printers' Arms Inn in Tottington centre. The coroner, J. Broughton Edge, swore in a jury, then promptly adjourned until Monday 14 August, 'to enable a post-mortem examination to be carried out'.

At this, the *Bury Times* newspaper fell into error. In reporting the reasons why the coroner was said to have taken this action, their issue for Saturday 12 August had this to say: '… about three years ago, two deaths occurred in the same family, of children about the same age and in similar circumstances. The parents were then censured by the coroner, Mr Dearden. It is the frequency of deaths, and the similarity, that has led Mr J. Broughton Edge to adjourn the inquest and order a post mortem.' This startling report was not contested until a fortnight later, but for convenience the objection can be dealt with now.

An unnamed member of the coroner's jury at a later stage of the inquest produced a copy of the offending report and also cuttings from earlier issues of the same newspaper, in which obituary notices on two other members of the Hutton family were recorded. The reports were quite contradictory, he complained. The obituaries disclosed that on 18 February 1853 – eighteen years before – a three-year-old child named Hutton was interred at St Anne's Church, Tottington, and on 6 January 1866 – five years before – another Hutton child had been interred in the same place. There was no suggestion in either case that death was other than natural, and no reference to any censure from the coroner.

In their issue of Saturday 26 August 1871 a chastened *Bury Times* carried an acknowledgement of the error and an apology.

I have some sympathy with the *Bury Times*. They had got the information from 'a reliable source', they explained, and had published it in good faith. Perhaps they had – and perhaps there was truth in it. After all, J. Broughton Edge must have had some reason for ordering a post mortem – by no means a matter of course in those days. And it is recorded that, when addressing the jury at the resumed inquest, he stated, 'As you know, I was not satisfied with the cause of death …'

If Mrs Scholes is to be believed, the call for a post-mortem was welcome news to the parents of the dead boy. 'They were very distressed and puzzled,' she said. 'As soon as he was dead, his mother said to me, "We shall have to tell Reuben [PC Barton]. There will have to be a 'Crowner's' inquest on it. I hope they will 'open' the child".'

The post mortem was performed on Friday 11 August, 'some fifty-six hours after the death', by Dr Harris, assisted by Drs Crompton and Ashworth. Incongruously, by today's standards, it took place in the bedroom of the cottage at Brookside. PC Reuben Barton was present. He was to say later:

'As a result of something said to me by the doctors I went downstairs and spoke to the parents. I asked for the shirt Samuel had been wearing. Elizabeth Hutton said to me, "I don't know. Wherever it is, there was no spot on it." I had not mentioned anything about a spot at that time. Later she told me she had ripped it up and made away with it. I asked for the other clothes he had been wearing. She got them and I took possession of them. They appeared to have been washed. I also took possession of a black dress the mother was wearing, on which I noticed a stain.'

Confusion persisted about the shirt. The daughter, Alice Hutton, was to recall that her mother had torn up two shirts on the day Samuel died. 'She also tore up a shift. It was for the doctors.' Having said that, she corrected herself, explaining that the two shirts had been torn up 'on the day Sammy was opened'. 'It was because the doctors wanted cloths. One was my father's, the other our Andrew's.' And, indeed, a shirt was eventually produced which was said to be the one Samuel had been wearing. Alice identified it positively, saying she had made it for him.

Arising from what the doctors had discovered, on Saturday 12 August Superintendent Andrew Milne, head of Bury Division, went to the Huttons' house with PC Barton. This was not the cottage in Brookside but a 'new' house to which the family had moved immediately after the post-mortem. No address has been recorded, but evidence suggests it was near 'Stoney Brow', which is a few hundred yards further up Harwood Road.

When the officers arrived, the funeral guests were there, crowding in the house. In the superintendent's words, 'I told them I should have to postpone the funeral. I called James Hutton outside the house to speak with him. I said, "Do you know anything about oil of vitriol? You might know it better as sulphuric acid." He said, "I suppose it's poison." I asked him, "Have you got any in the house?" He replied, "No".'

The superintendent and James Hutton went into the cellar of the house, where Hutton handed Milne five bottles containing liquid substances. Afterwards, Milne told James and Elizabeth Hutton, 'You are being arrested for causing the death of your son, Samuel, by administering to him sulphuric acid or some other poisonous substance.'

James Hutton replied, 'If he has had anything, he has got it himself.' His wife said, 'He's surely not got to that stuff our Alice got to clean her gloves with?'

'I took the prisoners to Bury police station in my drag,' (a horse-drawn vehicle), the superintendent said. Asked if all this had happened at the new house, he added, 'The old house was quite empty at that time.'

Under the heading 'Suspected murder of a child by its parents', the *Bury Times* of Saturday 19 August reported that, 'James and Elizabeth Hutton, of Tottington, appeared before Bury Petty Sessions on Monday last, charged with causing the death of their son, aged 4, by poisoning. Mr Superintendent Milne told the magistrates that the child had died without a doctor being present. Following a post-mortem examination it appeared the child had died from poisoning and medical evidence would be called. He needed a week to investigate the case. They were remanded in custody.'

The same issue reported the second stage of the inquest, which was resumed at the Printers' Arms on Monday, 14 August, the jury answered to their names, then James and Elizabeth Hutton were brought into the room under police escort. After outlining the case, the coroner told the jury that the parents were now suspected of causing the child's death. He said, 'We will take the evidence of the surgeon and of Constable Barton, who received some clothing from the mother.'

When Dr Harris was called, some time was occupied in discussing the issuing of the makeshift death certificate. 'It's the first I have heard of a death certificate,' Milne said, and the coroner added, 'We must have it.' Eventually the doctor came to firmer ground and dealt with his post-mortem examination.

The child's body had been moderately plump and well nourished, he reported. There was no rigor mortis remaining.

On first examination he had noticed four or five brownish spots on the mouth and inside the lower lip. There was a thick white curdy fluid on the lips and gums and the membrane lining of the gullet. When he opened the body, he found the stomach blackened externally. Inside the stomach he found three to four ounces of a yellowish fluid on which he could see globules of an oily substance. There were black spots on the mucous lining of the stomach, so fixed as not to be removed by sponging. The left auricle and ventricle of the heart were empty, the right chambers filled with blood. The rest of the internal organs appeared normal.

Questioned by Superintendent Milne, he said: 'My opinion is that the death of the child has been caused by having taken some corrosive, irritant poison, most probably sulphuric acid. I have the contents of the stomach and the greater part of the gullet, windpipe and tongue in sealed vessels. They will have to be analysed to determine the substance.'

He was asked if he knew anything about the clothing worn by the dead child and replied, 'No. But I have been told the shirt was torn up.' The coroner then questioned him.

Coroner: 'In your opinion, was there any natural disease that might have caused death?'

Doctor: 'No. Not to account for the appearance of the mouth, throat and stomach.'

Coroner: 'And the cause was sulphuric acid?'

Doctor: 'Most likely sulphuric acid. The five brown stains round the mouth are such as would be likely if such a poison had been taken or administered. The stain at the side of the mouth would be by imbibation.'

Coroner: 'And if sulphuric acid were administered, what symptoms would you expect to follow?'

Doctor: 'Severe pain, followed by continual vomiting.'

Coroner: 'The curdy appearance would indicate pain?'

Doctor: 'Yes – and vomiting. But I don't think the strongest acid can have been imbibed, or the appearances would have been more marked. However, whatever the strength, imbibing the acid would cause pain. The child would remain

	conscious until almost the last; then, as death approached, he would sink into a state of indifference – quiescence. His breathing would be quick and short. The muscles of the face would be slightly convulsed.'
Coroner:	'Did you find any sign of bread and butter in the stomach?'
Doctor:	'No. No solids. Liquid. Tea leaves. Possibly the bread and butter had dissolved.'

It was 5.30 p.m. by the time the doctor finished his evidence, and J. Broughton Edge then addressed the jury.

'Well, gentlemen. We can go no further today. I had thought of hearing Constable Barton's evidence but there is no time, so I propose to adjourn to next Wednesday week, the 23rd instant. That will allow time for police enquiries and analysis of the stomach contents. Also stains on the child's jacket and on the bedroom floor. These two,' he went on, indicating the accused, 'are now in custody and will remain so.'

At that stage occurred the first clear sign that public opinion was rapidly hardening in favour of Mr and Mrs Hutton. The flow of sympathy was to become a flood in the days that followed, but Josiah Hutchinson, a member of the jury, was responsible for starting it. Rising from his seat, he demanded: 'Cannot bail be considered?'

'Oh, certainly not,' the coroner replied. By now he must have been wondering how impartial were the jury he had empanelled.

The refusal was accepted but it did not please the jury, and indirectly it may have sparked off the next event: the jury joined forces to demand payment for their labours. J. Broughton Edge turned the demand down flat. The jury persisted, pointing out that expenses had been paid at other trials. This was not a trial but an inquiry, they were told. When the exchange was becoming heated, the coroner settled the argument by saying that it was not his responsibility and they should make their application to 'the proper quarter', though he did not specify where the proper quarter might be.

The rebellion ended. The prisoners were taken from the room under escort and thence to Bury police station by cab. But this was achieved only with difficulty, due to 'a remarkable scene' which took place outside the Printers' Arms.

'There was great excitement in the neighbourhood,' the *Bury Times* reported. 'A large crowd had gathered and there was weeping and angry language as the grown-up daughter of the prisoners was being carried away in a paroxysm of despair. A crowd besieged Mr Superintendent Milne opposite the public house and some of them showed a desire to lynch him. One bystander was heard to remark on "the utter improbability of a woman who had brought up ten children poisoning any of them".'

On the following day, Tuesday 15 August, some 500 well-wishers attended a meeting in the main hall of St John's Free School, Tottington. Their purpose was to devise a means of raising funds for the defence and in particular to provide proper legal aid for the Huttons. The Reverend John Brunskill took the chair and had no difficulty in rallying support. After preliminary discussions the meeting was adjourned, to be reconvened on the following Thursday in the hall of the Wesleyan School, Tottington.

There was much activity in the meantime.

On the day following the arrest, Superintendent Milne and Constable Barton visited the cottage at Brookside – the old house – and carried out a search. They took possession of three bottles, selected from a quantity found in the cellar. When asked later why he had selected those particular bottles, Milne replied: 'Because they had something in.'

They found a great many stains on the floor of the bedroom, and Milne brought in a local joiner and had him cut out two stained sections of the floor. Part of the flagged floor in the downstairs room also appeared to be stained, and one of the flagstones was lifted and removed. Constable Barton then took the bottles from the old and new houses, the two pieces of floorboard, the flagstone, the clothes worn by the dead child and the black dress worn by the child's mother to Bury, where he handed them over to Dr Harris. The clothing included a shirt which the mother now said was the one Samuel had been wearing. It had been washed since the boy's death, and the next youngest child, David, had been wearing it.

Later the same day the constable collected the articles from the doctor's surgery, together with a number of sealed glass vessels containing body parts, and delivered all of them to the laboratory of Frederick Grace Calvert PD, FRSP, who practised as an analytical chemist in Manchester. Dr Calvert was sufficiently interested in the stained floorboards to visit the Brookside cottage himself and remove a further fourteen pieces of the bedroom floor.

On Thursday 17 August the Reverend Mr Brunskill held his second supporters' meeting at the Wesleyan School. He reported that William Hoyle, a mill-owner, of Bury, had on his own responsibility and at his own expense engaged Mr Anderton, solicitor, of Bury, to watch the case on behalf of the accused. Superintendent Milne had allowed Anderton to interview the prisoners, and he had obtained depositions from them, on the strength of which he hoped eventually to brief a barrister.

Thus when the inquest was resumed at the Printers' Arms on Wednesday 23 August Anderton was present to observe the proceedings. As it happened, they were quite short. The coroner announced that Dr Calvert, of Manchester, who was making an analysis, had not yet completed his work, so a further adjournment for one week was necessary. Anderton immediately applied for bail on behalf of his clients, but this was bluntly refused. The following is just a sample of a long exchange.

Anderton: 'We can put up the most substantial bail.'
Coroner: 'No.'
Anderton: 'And we have a complete answer to the charge.'
Coroner: 'No.'

This was the session at which a juror raised the issue of the 'two previous deaths' as a result of which the *Bury Times* had later to print a withdrawal and apology.

Also at this session, before adjourning, the coroner proposed that the venue should be changed to the police court at Bury, which was 'altogether more convenient'. It was so for him – and for the police and Mr Anderton – but not for the jury. They vetoed it.

'Very well then,' the coroner snapped. 'It will be here. This day week.'

The coroner was not to be totally defeated. When he again took his seat, on Wednesday 30 August, he announced firmly that the venue would be moved forthwith to St John's Free School, which would better allow the public to watch the proceedings. There was much grumbling from the jury, but the coroner had his way.

The distance from the Printers' Arms to St John's Free School is about half a mile, and though the exodus is nowhere described, one can imagine the noisy procession of coroner, jury, witnesses, prisoners and police passing along the main street, which no doubt was lined with sightseers, many of them hostile. Among the throng were various dignitaries, including Mr Cottingham, a barrister, who had by now been briefed to represent the Huttons.

But there was one face absent, that of James Robinson, a member of the jury who had failed to show up. Whilst expressing his regret in penalizing a man who was unemployed and most likely could ill afford the loss, Broughton Edge announced that the recognizance of £10 under which Robinson had been bound would be estreated. In the event, the missing juror turned up as the inquest was in progress. He said he had now obtained work in Manchester but had missed his train at Manchester Victoria Station. The only bus he could catch had brought him as far as Prestwich and he had been obliged to walk on from there. The distance from Prestwich is some seven miles – eight, by the time Robinson had walked to the Printers' Arms and back to the new venue – and on the strength of this effort the coroner withdrew the estreatment and allowed Robinson to rejoin the jury.

Almost immediately afterwards the jury was again reduced by one. It now appeared that juror Harry Lomax, who had officiated at all sessions so far, would be required to give evidence. Today, no doubt, the entire jury would be replaced and a fresh start made, but Lomax was discharged and the inquest continued.

Various witnesses were called and their statements need be dealt with only fairly briefly.

John Hutton said he was twenty-one years old and the eldest child of his parents. Until five months earlier he had lived with the family but now he was married and lived near the Red Lion

Inn. He worked at Tottington Mill. He had gone to Brookside after work on Tuesday 8 August and seen his young brother, Sammy. He often played with the little fellow. Sammy was sitting on his mother's knee. 'He seemed all right, but drowsy. He was dressed in a little striped jacket, waistcoat and trousers, all in matching fustian cloth. These are the garments produced in court. My parents were always very good to me: to all of us. During the following night I was called back to the house by my brother, Andrew. Sammy was dead. My father had gone to Bury, seeking a doctor.'

John said his family had now left the Brookside cottage. Before them, a painter had lived there. He was William Scholes, who now lived next door. He used to keep paints there. John had seen no bottles belonging to Scholes. His father had no bottles – in the cellar or elsewhere.

Questioned by Mr Cottingham, he said Sammy had not seemed to be in pain. He had not vomited. He had only asked to go to bed.

Alice Jane Hutton said she worked as a hooker-on at the Bleach-croft. On the afternoon of the day of his death she had seen her brother Samuel playing with other children behind a pigsty near the new house at which they were now living but had not been at the time. She saw nothing the matter with him. Later he was lying on the sofa and asked her for a 'butty', which she made but he did not eat. He drank half a cup of tea.

Questioned by the coroner and others, she added: 'I slept with my brothers, Thomas and David, at Brookside. There was only one bedroom in the house. My parents and Sammy slept in another bed in the same room and my other brothers in a third bed. When my mother called me to the sick child, he was hot and poorly but not vomiting. There was no vomit on the floor or in any of the three chamber pots in the room. He did not twitch his mouth – he moved his mouth and ground his teeth. He was not dressed then, but wrapped in a blanket. I put the clothes he had been wearing into a dolly-tub to steep. I saw no stains on the clothing. I was away fetching water from the well when he died.'

As mentioned earlier, Alice spent some time dealing with the shirt, and with other shirts torn up, 'for the doctors'.

'When I saw him playing near the pigsty, there were a lot of bottles about. Also in Harry Lomax's cart. Harry Lomax carts away old things.'

At this point Harry Lomax was discharged from the jury and told he would be called to give evidence later.

Continuing, Alice Hutton described the positions of the beds in the one bedroom. She had not noticed a large stain at the foot of her parents' bed. She knew pieces had been cut from the bedroom floor. She knew there had been many stains but she could not remember details. She had often scrubbed the bedroom floor, using caustic soda in water. Her parents, she said, had always treated all their children very kindly.

Thomas Hutton presented the court with problems. He did not know how old he was but was 'over ten'. He could not read or write or say the Lord's Prayer – and he had never heard of God. He did know, however, that he would be punished if he lied, and on that basis his evidence was admitted. This witness was evidently very confused. He said he worked at the print-works from 6 a.m. to 8 p.m. daily, except Saturday and Sunday, and on Saturday he worked from 5 a.m. to 1 p.m.

Coroner:	'How long have you been doing that?'
Thomas:	'A year.'
Coroner:	'At ten years old? That is scandalous.'

But once more a member of the jury chipped in to point out that Thomas was still attending school. That was right, Thomas agreed. He was a 'half-timer'.

The boy's evidence was not particularly helpful. He had seen Sammy several times, playing near the new house, but could not remember much about it. He knew of no stains, no vomit, no complaints of illness. But his parents were always good to him.

Mr Cottingham thought he had heard enough by now. 'There is no evidence so far against the accused,' he said.

Coroner:	'I agree. But there are sixteen more witnesses.'
Milne:	'And two more. Doctors Calvert and Harris.'

It was agreed to call a few more witnesses before adjourning.

William Hutton said he was eleven years old and worked at the smithy. On the day of the death, when he came home from work, 'I washed myself outside the door, then went out to play. I saw Sammy. He was sick. I mean ill, not throwing up. I saw no vomit. I had seen him earlier, playing up near Stoney Brow, near the new house.' In common with his siblings, William said his parents had always been very good to him, and to the others.

Charles Hutton, aged fifteen, said he was a plater-down at the Bleach-croft. He had seen Sammy lying on the sofa, undressed but wrapped in a blanket. He had seen no stains on the floor, and no vomit. One of the chamber pots had something in it, but it was not vomit. His parents were always good and kind.

Andrew Hutton, nineteen, was a back-tenter at the printworks. He was out at work all day. He saw Sammy only in the evening, on the sofa. He might have been asleep or awake. He just lay quiet. His parents had always been very good to him.

Andrew was almost the final witness of the day. The exception was Alice, recalled to the stand by Mr Cottingham. In reply to his question she said, 'My father has been Paymaster for the Foresters for a very long time.'

Cottingham:	'Has not he been re-elected to that position since being taken up?' (Arrested.)
Coroner:	'You are trying to put in evidence of character. I cannot allow character evidence in. This is not a trial, but an inquest.'

He then adjourned until Wednesday 6 September.

On that date Mrs Scholes was first witness. Her evidence has largely been dealt with, but she added: 'We occupied that cottage before the Huttons. My husband kept turpentine, oil, white lead and paint in the upstairs bedroom. There were stains on the floor.'

Coroner:	'Describe those stains.'
Mrs Scholes:	'Oh, I couldn't possibly do that. It was more than five years ago when we moved out.'

Mrs Jane Shaw said she lived next door to the Huttons, on the other side from the Scholes's. Called to the deathbed she washed the child's body. He was stout in body. She saw no marks or stains around his mouth or lips.

Coroner:	'But at the post mortem there were plain marks.'

Mrs Shaw: 'I never saw any, and I would have if there had been any.'

She could not be shaken in this denial. After a spell of fencing she added that the Huttons were good, kind parents who always treated their children well.

Police Constable Barton and Superintendent Milne gave evidence in turn, most of which has already been outlined. The superintendent was subjected to a long cross-examination by Mr Cottingham, which included this rather surprising exchange:

Cottingham: 'Did you ask them to confess?'
Milne: 'Never.'
Cottingham: 'Rumour has it otherwise.'
Milne: 'I would never do that.'
Coroner: 'I know Mr Superintendent Milne as an honourable man. He would not do such a thing.'
Cottingham: 'I agree. It was just a rumour. I have it from the accused that he did not do so.'

Dr Calvert then gave evidence and produced various exhibits: a jar containing the whole of the deceased's intestines, liver and heart; a jar containing the gullet and tongue; the child's clothing; the mother's black dress; the flagstone and sixteen pieces of boarding cut from the bedroom floor. He said: 'I treated all the organs with pure, strong alcohol. I mixed the resultant solution with water and evaporated it to the consistency of syrup. I then applied one of the best tests we know for sulphuric acid. I wrote on paper with the solution, then applied gentle heat. The writing blackened as the paper charred.'

This test was positive, he said, as were several other tests. He also confirmed sulphuric acid by use of litmus paper. The doctor went on at great length to describe finding traces of sulphuric acid in the stains on some, though not all, of the pieces of floorboard. There was, however, '... not much product from the stains. They were mainly sulphates, ammonia, dirt and urine. And there was not as much sulphuric acid in the stomach as I would have expected to find. There were slight traces of sulphuric acid on some of the clothing. Nothing on the flagstone.' His findings, he thought, were inconclusive, '... except that the cause of death was undoubtedly by sulphuric acid poisoning'.

Mr Cottingham seized on this. 'At the moment,' he said, 'there is nothing that inculpates these two people.'

Coroner:	'Possibly not. But it seems to me there is a case – a shadow of one.'
Cottingham:	'Well, coming events cast their shadows. Is there anything to come after the shadows? Has Superintendent Milne any more witnesses to call?'
Coroner:	'I should like to know if *you* have any witnesses you would like me to call.'
Cottingham:	'If the witnesses to be called by the police are all called, I should ask what possible reason there is for calling my witnesses, because I see no case.'
Coroner:	'I must leave that to the jury.'
Cottingham:	'There is not a judge in England who would let this case go before a jury.'
Coroner:	'Doctor Harris is to come. I do not know what his evidence is.'

There followed a heated argument in which Mr Cottingham sought to call Dr Harris straight away and be done with it, but the coroner pleaded strain and pressure of other work.

Cottingham:	'There is no scintilla of evidence. Doctor Harris can throw no further light on it.'
Coroner:	'I think he can. This inquest is adjourned until Friday the 8th September.'

The prisoners came up for further remand at Bury Petty Sessions on Thursday 7 September, but this time only for two days.

'I have no wish to keep them in longer than necessary,' the superintendent told the magistrates, 'but the inquest has been adjourned until tomorrow.'

At the resumed inquest on the Friday, the Reverend John

Brunskill, chairman of the well-wishers' committee, took an active and apparently unexpected hand in the proceedings. Called to the stand, he produced a green cider bottle with the neck broken off, which he said had been found in the brook near the pigsty by the Huttons' new house. Asked how he had been put on to it, he explained that the matter had come up at one of his fund-raising meetings on behalf of the defence. A boy called John Thomas Wilkinson had told him about it. He had then directed Robert Greenhalgh to go into the brook and bring the bottle to him. Eventually he had handed the bottle to the police (that very day, reading between the lines) but first he had tested the bottle, using litmus paper, and obtained an acid reading. He had then kept the bottle in a drawer for 'some time' before handing it over, but it was in the same condition as when he had received it from Robert Greenhalgh. Surprisingly, no criticism seems to have been made of Brunskill's actions.

Robert Greenhalgh, a finisher at the Tottington Mill, confirmed this testimony. The brook, he said, ran past the house where the Huttons now lived and also past the Brookside house, where it was culverted, to reappear again near the Printers' Arms. He had found the bottle some fifty yards upstream of the old house, lying on its side and half filled with water. After teeming the water out, he handed the bottle to the Reverend Brunskill.

John Thomas Wilkinson proved to be five years old, and the coroner admitted his evidence only '... with reluctance, since if this matter appears before another court it may well be excluded'.

Reluctantly admitted or not, what the boy had to say must have given the assembly fresh food for thought. He remembered playing with Sammy, '... the last time up near Old Harry's, with Tom Seddon and Willy Lomax. We were playing marbles. There were some bottles in Old Harry's cellar. I didn't go in, but Sammy went in. He supped out of this bottle, then threw it in the brook.'

Questioned, he said Sammy had vomited three times. When asked what he thought was in the bottle, he replied, to much laughter: 'Peysen.' (Poison.)

Willy Lomax, aged six, confirmed that Sammy had drunk out of the bottle, and added in his innocence, 'John-Tommy made him.'

'Old Harry' was, of course, the discharged juror, Harry Lomax. He took the stand but his evidence was brief and inconclusive. There were numbers of old bottles lying about his premises but he had no idea what was in them.

Annoyingly, we shall never know what was in the cider bottle. There is no record that it was ever submitted for analysis.

James Tootill said he was manager of the grey-room at Mr Whowell's bleach works and also Secretary of the Bradshaw Funeral Society. The deceased had been a member of the society. On the day following the boy's death, James Hutton had approached him. He was certain Hutton had told him the boy had died from sunstroke, and there had been some hot days around that time. He had issued a certificate authorizing the father to collect the money due to him on the death. The amount was £2.10s.

James Nuttall was Secretary of the Four Lane Ends Funeral Club. Samuel Hutton was not a member, but the other boy, David, was, and should David die, the family would be entitled to £1.10s.

The final witness, Dr Harris, had little to add to what he had said before. He had now seen the boy's clothing. There was a stain on the jacket but he did not think it was acid. The stains on the bedroom floor '... looked like acid. They were streaky stains as though caused by the cleaning up of vomit.'

Once again he gave as his opinion that the cause of the child's death was his having taken a corrosive poison which tests had now shown was sulphuric acid.

When the doctor had finished, Mr Cottingham expressed a wish to address the jury but the coroner would not permit it.

The coroner then addressed the jury himself.

All parties were satisfied, he said, that Samuel Hutton had died from sulphuric acid poisoning, and there was not a tittle of evidence otherwise. The questions remaining were when, how and by whom the poison had been administered. He advised them not to place too much weight on the evidence of the child witnesses. Their answers had been framed to suit questions and thus were not to be relied on.

On the medical evidence, the deceased must have vomited at some time, and if he had vomited, wouldn't the parents and others present have noticed signs of it? And if they had seen signs, why had they all denied it? The father had retracted part of his first account, and so had the daughter, Alice. Those diversities gave rise to grave suspicion that a false story had been concocted.

In the largest stain on the bedroom floor there had been free sulphuric acid, causing sulphate of ammonia in which as much as sixty grains of sulphuric acid had been found. It was a matter for them how it had got there ...

After reviewing the whole of the evidence, he closed by advising the jury that, if they had any doubt at all, they should stop short of a verdict of wilful murder.

If the coroner's summing-up was against the Huttons, as seems evident, it made no impression on the jury – or perhaps they had made their minds up long before. They retired for only twenty minutes before returning to announce their verdict.

'We find,' the foreman said, 'that the child has died from poison, but which way it has got to it is unknown, and the opinion of all the jury is that the parents are innocent.'

The announcement was followed by immediate applause from the public benches, but this was quickly quelled. The coroner then asked shortly: 'What poison?'

'Sulphuric acid,' the foreman replied.

Cottingham:	'I shall ask you in announcing the result to include the rider that the parents are innocent.'
Coroner:	'You know I can't do that.'

After more pressing, Cottingham conceded the point, but he added: 'I shall ask that they be released immediately.'

Superintendent Milne:	'That is perfectly arranged.'
Cottingham:	'I presume we shall still have to go to Bury?'
Milne:	'That is so.'

The verdict of the coroner's jury was greeted with great public excitement and acclaim. 'Loud cheering and huzzahs,' reported the *Bury Times*, 'were heard from Tottington all the way to Bury Bridge.' But an editorial in the same issue of the newspaper advised caution amid all the euphoria. 'We know we are skating on thin ice, but ...', the editorial began, and it went on to point out that the case was not over, the verdict not final, until consideration had been given to proceeding with the trial in another court.

On the following day James and Elizabeth Hutton were once more remanded at Bury Petty Sessions. This time, however, they were released on bail.

There followed an uneasy interval of sixteen days. Although the fact is not recorded, there can be no doubt that during those sixteen days the case papers were submitted to the Public Prosecutor – and it seems likely that his advice was against going on with the case. Certainly Superintendent Milne seems to have given up any thought of doing so.

On Monday 25 September 1871 James and Elizabeth Hutton answered to their bail at Bury Petty Sessions before Messrs T.L. Openshaw and Jesse Leach, lay magistrates. Superintendent Milne asked that bail be ended on the grounds that the case would not be continued.

'You are discharged,' the accused were told.

Walking out of Bury Court, they were once more greeted by cheering crowds anxious to congratulate them on their vindication.

They passed thence into obscurity.

Index